Healing the Heart

HEALING THE HEART

A THERAPEUTIC APPROACH TO DISTURBED CHILDREN IN GROUP CARE

Alvin Rosenfeld, M.D.
Saul Wasserman, M.D.

Child Welfare League of America
Washington, DC

CHILD WELFARE LEAGUE OF AMERICA, INC.
440 First Street, NW, Suite 310, Washington, DC 20001

CURRENT PRINTING (last digit)
10 9 8 7 6 5 4 3 2 1

Cover design by Chad Bruce
Text design by Eve Malakoff-Klein

Printed in the United States of America

ISBN # 0-87868-391-7

In loving memory
of my mother,
Sara Lee Rosenfeld

Contents

PREFACE

This monograph grew out of a collaboration that began in 1977. One of us (Dr. Alvin A. Rosenfeld) became Stanford University's Director of Child Psychiatry training. As part of his teaching responsibilities, he consulted to the Child and Adolescent Psychiatric Inpatient Unit (CAPI) of San Jose Hospital, teaching residents who rotated through the unit and discussing their progress with its new director, Dr. Saul Wasserman. In our discussions, we found that both of us had a deep interest in a group of children that child psychiatrists had tended to ignore up until then, relatively speaking. We were interested in finding better ways to heal these children's wounds.

We began to discuss our experiences and to talk about children we had known or were seeing in our daily clinical practice. Out of these discussions, and other activities related to child abuse, we began to understand these children better and developed a clearer picture of what needed to be done to treat them more successfully.

Over the years, both of us were profoundly influenced by a beloved teacher and friend, Dr. Bruno Bettelheim, who had retired in Palo Alto and who became both an active teacher in the child psychiatry training program and subsequently a clinical consultant at CAPI. Dr. Bettelheim taught us much that he had learned about severely disturbed children in his 30 years as the director of the Sonia Shankman Orthogenic School of the University of Chicago. We found that many of the approaches he had originally developed for work with autistic and psychotic children were particularly useful in restoring severely maltreated children to emotional health.

We consider this work crucial to the children as individuals and to society as a whole. The children's wounds need to be healed so that they can live good productive lives, and also so that our society can be spared the damage these children are prone to inflict on themselves and the revenge they take on others if they are not well treated and healed.

Dr. Wasserman has remained at Stanford University and at the CAPI Unit, where he continues his interest in child abuse from both a clinical and social policy perspective. Most recently, he has been involved in projects concerning maltreatment-related death analysis and programs oriented toward severely abused chronic runaways. Dr. Rosenfeld has become the director of psychiatric services at the Jewish Child Care Association in New York and a senior research scholar at the Ellenwood Center of Columbia University's Teacher College. He has continued his work and writing on child abuse, healthy forms of parenting and, with Dr. Bettelheim, on psychotherapy. Both of us have applied our understandings and treatment principles to residential treatment centers, group homes, and foster homes.

Our views and approaches have not been universally accepted with joy. We are both familiar with the arguments clinicians and administrators, as well as some who shape governmental policy, make about an approach that emphasizes using a deeper understanding of what drives these children's behavior as a foundation for treating them.

Resistance to this approach is understandable. The work we describe is not easy; anyone undertaking it needs to be deeply committed to repairing the damage that cruel, indifferent, self-centered, or inadequate parents have inflicted. The work involves dealing with children who are extraordinarily emotionally and intellectually demanding. Furthermore, our approach will not work with every child and cannot be applied easily to every program, particularly at a time when the well-being of children ranks so low as a social and economic priority, and when we mortgage our future by investing proportionally so little in the next generation.

Our experience has convinced us that the approach we describe has a greater likelihood of producing long-term attitudinal, personality, and behavioral change than simpler and more mechanistic behaviorist strategies. Furthermore, in our experience the approach ultimately leads to work that is more gratifying to the clinicians involved in treatment. This may diminish the huge staff turnover at many residential treatment centers, which would itself benefit the children. In the long run, we believe that the savings to society will far outweigh the additional expenditures that have to be made to adequately staff and fund excellent therapeutic facilities.

Our medical training has emphasized that we treat a disorder best if we understand its origin and provide as specific a remedy for the defect as is possible. In a way, these children suffer from a deficiency disease. Their lives have not given them nurturance and enough experience with positive and stable human relationships for them to join society willingly and to live well in it. The dilemma that treating them presents is that any sensitive clinician who tries to learn about the unique and terrible experiences these children have had tends to be overwhelmed just by hearing about their lives and imagining what it was like to endure so much suffering.

A wise man once said that God is in the details. Understanding the details of these children's lives is essential to treating them successfully. Before coming into care these children have failed miserably in human relationships; their efforts to evoke from their parents the love and care they need to thrive psychologically and to flourish emotionally have been greeted with hostility (child abuse) or gross indifference (neglect). This is the generic insult that causes their illness. Although we consider the parents at fault for this failure, social policy often reflects our society's concurrence with the view that the children, or their disturbing behavior, and not their upbringing or terrible experiences, are to blame.

A treatment facility that treats these children must regard each as precious and unique so that their hearts can be healed and they can come to live a good life. Only through careful observation of each child can the particular insults and deficiencies the child suffered be understood. Only with this insight can the treatment team devise the unique interventions that persuade the child that he or she has worth and the hope for a better future. The challenge is to find a creative way to give each child a new chance for stable, restorative relationships in a setting that must serve many children at once. We emphasize that the process takes time and is demanding. Our experience, however, has been that the creative energy invested in understanding and helping these children is richly rewarded over time. As an old Jewish saying tells us, anyone who saves a single life has as good as saved the whole world.

The treatment approach for these children needs to be cut from a single cloth; each of its component parts are important to the whole process. We have used the term "therapist" to describe a person, typically a social worker, psychologist, or child psychiatrist, trained in providing psychotherapy. In the treatment programs we are describing, each child receives individual therapy several times a week. Family sessions may occur frequently, intermittently, or not at all. In coordination with the child care staff, the therapist also may provide the case management and develop the child's treatment plan. The child care staff comprises those individuals who provide the parenting for the children. They have been specially trained in psychological principles, with a focus on understanding and responding to the children in ways that will further the children's growth. Since they live with the children, they are crucial in giving them the direct experiential learning that creates growth. The goal is to create a specific environment and relationships in which learning can occur throughout the day as the children try to negotiate the tasks of daily living.[1] We consider this living situation "therapeutic." At times we have used the term "clinicians" as a general term for all those adults who adhere to these goals when they interact with the child, either in therapy or in the therapeutic environment.

We hope that the explanations, approaches, and examples we use in this monograph will help all those who work with maltreated children to deal with them more sympathetically and effectively. We encourage you to look honestly at your feelings. No one feels benevolent all the time, especially to these provocative children. Your own anger can become an important tool that can help you form a relationship with a disturbing child. Your skill in understanding can help solve problems. The children will learn more from what you actually do with them, particularly when the going gets rough, than they ever learn from what you tell them to do.

These children are numerous. Many intelligent, well-intentioned people need to work hard if we are ever to heal the wounds their young hearts have sustained at a very tender age. We hope that others will supplement these ideas so that with time we all can become wiser in our understanding, more precise in our interventions, and more potent in our therapeutic efforts.

We would like to thank Carl Schoenberg of the Child Welfare League of America for his cooperation and editorial assistance.

Alvin A. Rosenfeld, M.D.
New York City, New York

Saul Wasserman, M.D.
Palo Alto, California

Notes

1 See Redl and Wineman, *Controls From Within* (New York: Free Press, 1965) for an extensive discussion of this approach.

I

The Population of Children

This monograph sets forth certain approaches to initiating treatment with severely disturbed and disturbing children who, on closer study, turn out to have been seriously mistreated, usually at the hands of their parents. "Mistreatment" means that these children have endured frightening, painful experiences, such as having been frequently abandoned, beaten, burned, starved, raped, or in other ways sexually exploited. In response to this kind of mistreatment, some children develop behavioral disturbances so severe that if they do not improve with treatment, society may isolate them permanently from the general population.[1] Many observers have pointed out that severe mistreatment in childhood is frequently associated with adult antisocial, deviant, or criminal behavior.[2]

Although individual children respond to mistreatment in various ways, those described here have reacted with marked aggressive or destructive behavior, turned outward or inward. They may assault adults in authority, such as teachers, or they may vandalize property or set fires. If their rage is directed outward they may attack or even attempt to murder others. Terms such as oppositional, resistive, explosive, conduct-disordered, or disrespectful of adult authority are used to describe them. They may direct their rage inward and injure themselves or attempt suicide. Other children in this group show their disturbance in sexually precocious, aggressive, or assaultive behavior directed toward either adults or other children.

Some of these severely disturbed children are admitted to a child psychiatric hospital because they are considered too difficult to treat elsewhere. Even after a period of hospitalization, therapeutically oriented residential settings may find some of these children too difficult to cope with. In the first half of this monograph we focus on the nature of the mistreatment, its impact on the child's developing world view, and the behavioral problems that it creates. The second half deals with clinical issues that beset the therapists who seek to restore the children to emotional health. All the illustrative examples are derived from clinical experience.

Notes

1 Certainly not all abused children become delinquent, mentally ill, or drug abusers, certainly not all delinquents, mentally ill persons, or drug abusers have been seriously mistreated as children. On the other hand, the correlations are significant. See Judge Betty Friedlander, "A Case for Preventive Criminal Justice" (Ithaca, NY: Family Court, Tompkins County).

2 Bolton, F.G.; Reich, J.W.; and Guitierres, S.E.,"Delinquent Patterns in Maltreated Children and Siblings," *Victimology* 2 (1977): 349; Lewis, D.O., "Neuropsychiatric Vulnerabilities and Violent Juvenile Delinquency," *Psychiatric Clinics of North America* 6 (1983): 707; Lewis, D.O.; Shanosk, S.S.; Pincus, J.H.; and Glaser, G.H., "Violent Juvenile Delinquents: Psychiatric, Neurological, Psychological, and Abuse Factors," *Journal of the American Academy of Child Psychiatry* 18 (1979): 307; Hunner, R.J., and Walker, Y.E., eds., *Exploring the Relationship between Child Abuse and Delinquency* (1981); Martin, H.P., "The Consequences of Being Abused and Neglected: How the Child Fares," in *The Battered Child* (3rd ed.), ed. C.H. Kempe and R.E. Helfer (1980).

II

The Nature of the Problem

Adults have great emotional difficulty in fully understanding, taking to heart, and integrating the painful events in these children's lives and the impact these experiences have had on their personality development. Some reasons for this difficulty seem pragmatic. Formal, unequivocal proof of the extent of maltreatment may be difficult to obtain. The histories that caregivers or social welfare agencies give usually include only sketchy information. In an effort to be accurate and avoid challenge in court, or to facilitate a tentative truce with an angry, uncooperative, defensive parent, professionals often word court reports carefully and water down facts so that only sketchy information is included. The clinicians developing the children's treatment program may have great difficulty forming a clear, accurate picture of what actual insults and abuse the children have endured. When clinicians are able to contact relatives, neighbors, visiting nurses, and other observers to get a clearer picture, they are likely to discover that the child has suffered treatment far more harsh and severe, far more cruel and sadistic, than referral court social workers felt free to commit to writing.

But personal reasons may also interfere with the therapist's and caretakers' ability to empathize. These children have been treated in ways that are drastically different from what most of us have experienced during our own childhood. Adults tend to match the children's experience against their own, reaching into their feelings and past, trying to visualize the children's world both to understand it and to build an empathic bond with them. As a starting point in trying to appreciate how child patients feel about the world, clinicians rely a great deal on recollections of their own childhood. But to understand the cruel yet actual life experiences these children have lived through demands that the adults open their hearts to a difficult and internally unpleasant process. They must imagine the horrifying. For instance, they must visualize the sight, smells, and feelings a son experienced when his father put out a cigarette on his son's arm. To empathize with that child's experience, clinicians must rethink many of the everyday views they developed from their own often relatively good, usually middle-class upbringings and experiences. The popular image that childhood is a period of happy, protected, carefree innocence may not be accurate for many of those who enter child welfare as a profession. If it does hold, it may be tarnished by memories of unhappy experiences or by the recollections recaptured in a personal analysis. But few clinicians we know have experienced their own childhood as an unending nightmare filled with violence and violation. In trying to understand a world in which unrelieved and fully justified fear reigns, in which the threat that your parent will kill you or violate you sexually is an everyday occurrence, clinicians are forced to confront processes related to their own psychological maturation and painful, suppressed recollections and feelings.

We fear pain, abandonment, and death and go to great lengths to avoid them. We try to construct a life in which we feel safe and loved, or at least not endangered or abandoned. As part of our psychological development, we develop ways to protect ourselves from the unbearable anxiety associated with external danger; for self-protection we suppress many unpleasant childhood experiences. In contrast, these mistreated children have lived with physical danger, beatings, maimings, role reversal, abandonment, sexual stimulation, and family disorganization. They develop a view of the world and of human relationships that challenges any optimistic, self-protective image.

Although many of us view life, particularly in the big city, as potentially dangerous, and take precautions to avoid harm, for these children the danger is at home, from parents, whom we usually think of as every child's primary protectors. Having dangerous parents leaves these children without a secure base in the external world, so they cannot internalize a sense of security and carry it inside for the rest of their lives. To them, the world is neither in fact nor in potential a good place; their view is misanthropic from experience, and paranoid in defense. These children develop a picture of life as an unrelieved jungle, where every minor confrontation involves fighting, where being "lean, mean, and merciless" is the only way to survive.

In clinicians' efforts to remain in empathic contact with the parent (as the state mandates) and empathy with the adult world, they may have difficulty believing that what has been said about the children's experiences could actually have happened. We would like to believe that all parents really love children even if they don't know how to show it, and that it is not right for children to hate parents.

What real-life experiences produce these effects on children? A nine-year-old boy described how his father would urinate over him in the shower before sodomizing him. A 12-year-old showed the scar on his back where a stepfather carved his initials into the boy's back to show the boy's mother just who was in charge at home. A ten-year-old boy described how his mother choked him and threw him down a flight of stairs after she caught him taking cereal out of the refrigerator. Life on the streets may be safer and more gratifying than other options. As one 16-year-old prostitute put it, "I'd rather take my chances on the streets than having my stepfather rape me two or three times a week." For each of these children, the world is not only dangerous but also utterly destructive.

Empathizing with children who see even daily life at home as extremely dangerous, even life-threatening, propels clinicians into a situation of great insecurity that challenges our defenses and makes us anxious. Empathy with the children reawakens childhood fears and vulnerabilities, the sense of how close we were to being unprotected as children, and how frightening this possibility was. Advanced students, such as child psychiatry fellows, often go through an initial period of feeling overwhelmed and depressed by the harshness of the mistreated children's experience and by the severity of the damage. Later they may change from a stance of being angry at their own parents to better respecting the positive relationships in their own childhood.

The anxiety associated with the reappearance of primitive childhood fears may interfere with the clinician's ability to understand the children, to form an empathic connection, and to appreciate the children's needs. Within the mental health field this may be reflected by the use of vague and intellectual terms such as "The child needs to work through the trauma," or "The child needs to come to terms with what has happened." This language may serve primarily to protect therapists from the intellectually and emotionally difficult tasks involved in understanding the nature of the terror and what responses will help the child best survive.

Sometimes the failure to empathize is more overt. When a suicidal teenager was admitted to a state hospital, her assigned therapist told her to stop "sniveling" and "making up stories" when she described her stepfather raping her. She became even more depressed. Her mother and a previous therapist had to intervene to let the state hospital staff know that multiple witnesses had corroborated the girl's account. She was transferred to a new therapist and her mood gradually improved.

The problems with these children are more extensive than the clinicians' internal reactions. These children are very difficult to live with. Even clinicians who understand the children's plight and have empathy for their predicaments find the intensity of these children's emotional needs close to overwhelming. The children's intense sense that the world has deeply injured them is often manifested by a pervasive anger.[1] They are considered emotionally disturbed because they hate so thoroughly. Their deep sense that they have been deprived and their profound discouragement with themselves, with adults, with human relationships, and with life, make them very hard to satisfy.

Because they feel so deprived, they are often at their wits' end. Lacking emotional reserves, they in effect have hair-triggers that will fire with minimal pressure or frustration. Their angry feelings rapidly convert into violent behavior, directed toward any frustrating figure, adult or child. Unless the reasons for their violence are understood and factored into program planning, these children can rapidly stress parenting figures to the point where the adults lash back. Since the child is already convinced that the world is no good, this is doubly destructive. The surrogate parents' lashing out only validates the child's distorted view that all adults are cruel and unresponsive. It also supports their view that they can never be understood, perhaps because they are monsters.

For this reason, one basic precondition in initiating treatment is that staff members have control over the frustrations the children must face, and the program have control over the frustrations the staff must face, in order to keep the level of frustration low enough to avoid painful explosions. Yet many, if not most, treatment programs operate as part of a system that leads to the children, and sometimes the staff members, becoming overly frustrated, triggering the sequence outlined above. The treatment setting must cope with a variety of external pressures that interfere with its ability to respond therapeutically to these children. Economic resources may be severely limited, leading to the children again being forced to live in a deprived and depriving environment. If a child breaks a toy, no money may be available for a replacement, and the child may soon have no toys.

The psychological resources of the staff members may also be limited, either intrinsically or because the organization's leadership and outside funding agencies institute and enforce severe financial policies that make the staff feel frustrated and deprived. The children's deprivation inadvertently may come from staff members' feelings of resentment toward them— "With all we do, how dare the children expect more? After all, they brought it on themselves."[2]

Many institutions find it difficult to retain their focus on the children's needs. Any institution must serve staff needs as well as the needs of the children while being responsive to the outside world. In the welter of budget meetings, demands for cost-effective financing, insurance requirements, hospital, staff, university and board of trustee politics, individual ambitions, social pressures, and moral attitudes about "appropriate behavior," the concern with understanding and serving the children can easily be lost. Without persistent effort, the children's needs may be given little attention, particularly if the institution is large and the policy makers far removed from the daily clinical tasks. To make matters worse, clinicians may not acknowledge, even to themselves, how distressing this can be for their child patients. In an effort to keep the adult ranks united against the disruptive children and to provide an atmosphere of consistency, administrators may say to the children that policies made because of institutional needs *are* designed in the children's interest. This often is a rationalization.

As persons who are familiar with the problems of running large therapeutic institutions, we do not deny that certain policies must be made based on institutional, rather than individual, needs. But we are convinced that if the institution's mission is therapeutic, the children are better served if institutional needs are clearly labeled and dealt with as such. When decisions are made, the staff members can be more honest with themselves and with the children about why the decision was made; this helps preserve the sense of trust we want the children to develop.

For instance, many maltreated children feel that they are second-class or third-class persons, damaged goods lacking value and worth. Both at school and around other children in the community, the contrasts between children who have both parents and material goods and those who do not may be painful. But an attempt to treat the child in out-of-home care as "first-class" may be thwarted. Children in institutional care are frequently forced to live in circumstances far more austere than the environment in which the clinicians would raise their own children, even if they themselves were less financially advantaged.

A 12-year-old girl living in a group home complained bitterly because she was required to use generic shampoo, while the other children in her school had parents who bought name-brand products. The issue was discussed at a staff meeting. The initial staff reaction was that she should learn to use the generic shampoo, because it was thriftier. When the group was polled, however, not one of the six women in the group used generic shampoo, even though several were students on a limited budget. One staff member confessed that she had tried the cheaper brand but had stopped using it because, like the girl, she didn't like what it did to her hair. Careful examination showed that using a higher-quality shampoo would have only a miniscule impact the agency's budget, which was over one million dollars a year. In making their initial argument, the staff members had inadvertently accepted the view that this child was second-class, completely avoiding coming to grips with her feelings that she was unattractive, and not as valuable as the other children at her school. They had missed a concrete opportunity to help her with her low self-esteem. Had they responded to her feelings and provided the better shampoo, she would have felt more attractive, and they might have communicated at a deeper level that they considered her a valuable person and supported her efforts to be first-rate.

The third difficulty is that each child's experience is unique. As we noted above, in most cases accurate information is hard to get. But the child's behavior in out-of-home care often reflects an attempt to deal with experience in the past. Without an accurate history, clinicians have relatively little information to help them comprehend these purposes and goals in the child's behavior. Terms like "abuse" and "neglect" are generic entities, but give no information as to exactly how the child was mistreated, at what developmental point the insult occurred, and, most critically, what meaning the child ascribed to the abusive experience.

Some clinicians have trouble accepting that a child's behavior is purposeful. When the child misbehaves they might simply argue that the child was "seeking attention" or "acting out." Yet this behavior is often the child's way to return psychologically to their trauma in an attempt to master the abuse.[3] Only slowly, over time, do child and clinician come to comprehend the behavior's meaning and significance. When the clinician approaches the child with the attitude, "Under what circumstances would I act in this way? What would I be trying to achieve?" there is a far greater chance that the child will feel understood. Furthermore, the child will realize that the clinician is convinced that the child behaves in a certain way, however crazy or destructive it appears at first glance, for a good reason. That means that the child is a comprehensible human, not a monster. Once the message implicit in the symptom, which is chosen specifically rather than generically, is understood, the child usually can voluntarily change the offensive behavior.

For instance, what if a boy strongly refused to take a bath. Taking time to understand his behavior may interrupt the program's complex activity schedule. Should the schedule be interrupted? Is the child simply being negative or oppositional? It may take considerable adult patience, faith in the child, and faith in the viewpoint that people do not do things without good reason, to find out the truth. The facts usually embarrass the children because they see them as reflections of their badness; in sexual abuse cases children may consider the facts disgusting. In this particular case, it became clear with time that the bath terrified the boy because his mother had held his head under water and threatened to drown him as a disciplinary technique. He was ashamed to admit this, because he felt it reflected poorly on his family. Another child had a similar fear of showers. His father had sodomized and urinated on him while they showered together.

The clinicians' first task, then, is to understand more about the children's external world, and how it has shaped and defined their world view. Once a world view is understood, the clinicians can define a program that incorporates this understanding and furthers the child's socialization.

Deprivation, disorganization, violence, and loss have filled these children's lives. The next chapter will describe these experiences and discuss how they have affected the children, making them the kind of persons they are when they enter a treatment program.

Notes

1 Thus Redl and Wineman wrote about *Children Who Hate* (New York: Free Press, 1965).

2 Dickens' brilliant description of the children's orphanage in Oliver Twist has not lost its relevance 100 years later.

3 Lenore Terr has documented this well in her Chowchilla studies. Terr. L. "Children of Chowchilla: A Study of Psychic Trauma." *Psychoanalytic Study of the Child* 34 (1979): 547–62.

III

The Children's Lives Before Entering Treatment

Deprivation

By deprivation, we mean first not giving the physical elements that are necessary for life. In the adult world these are often referred to as food, clothing, and shelter.

In their daily lives, these children all too frequently suffer from hunger. Whether parents fail to respond to the children's need because of economic or psychological reasons, the children often do not have confidence that they will be fed consistently. The clinician frequently hears from them about episodes in which at first food is withheld to discipline them. Then they are punished severely for covertly taking food. In response and for protection, the children prudently assemble a reserve, a phenomenon called food hoarding.

The drive for food is a fundamental biological process. To emphasize feeding's neuropsychological primacy, Freud focused on orality as the first developmental stage. For mammals, more so for primates, and even more so for the human infant, soon after birth feeding becomes associated with the feeding figure, and thus the roots of human relatedness are established.

This process can go awry in many ways. Failure to feed children may sometimes be the reason they are removed from their home. We have seen several children whose parents severely beat them because they were caught stealing food. Only after a case where a parent killed a child in such a situation was analyzed retrospectively did the clinical scenario became apparent. In the few weeks and days before the episode, this parent, who was experiencing enormous stress and using illegal drugs, had been fighting with the child more and more frequently. Finally, to discipline the child, the parent sent the child to bed without dinner. In the early morning, when the child, by then very hungry, tried to sneak food, the parent exploded, with tragic results. We suspect that such a scenario is more common than most clinicians realize.

In these cases the impact of physical hunger on the children is hard to distinguish from the impact of emotional malnutrition. Failing to provide food clearly leads to malnourishment, but calories are not the only issue. These children's parents may supply adequate calories, but fail to establish even a rudimentary connection between eating and human contact. They may leave their infant child in a crib unattended with a bottle propped in the baby's mouth. Thus the pleasurable human contact and cuddling that are part of feeding for both parent and infant fail to be connected with the early feeding experience. When this occurs, the most fundamental building block of human relationship is not part of a neglected child's earliest experience.

Although failure to provide adequate calories is relatively easy to measure, assessing the emotional nutrition the child is given or deprived of is difficult. The later effects emotional malnutrition has are even harder to delineate. For example, a child may have an immature nervous system and be excessively irritable. This may lead the infant to reject an adult holding or stimulating him or her. If the parents are self-centered, immature, and sensitive to rejection, they may interpret the child's difficulty as a global rejection of them. Since they expect and rely on the child to make them feel good, they may see the child as hateful and not develop a loving relationship with the child.

Some mistreating parents fail to understand their child's biological eating rhythm or tempo. When this misunderstanding is severe, and the parents are frustrated or cruel, the child may be force fed, making eating aversive to the child.

If feeling secure includes feeling confident that one's needs will be met in an adequate and predictable way, we must conclude that these children are insecure at the most fundamental level. In response to deprivation, infants can lose faith and give up, as happens in marasmic babies, who despite adequate nutrition die from a lack of emotional nourishment.[1] Older children may figure out a way to fend for themselves without needing adults. When the children are starved they develop a world view and emotional outlook that says, "Adults won't respond to my hunger. Hence, I cannot trust them. I must fend for myself if I am to survive." In an Ericksonian sense, these children do not achieve basic trust,[2] infancy's most fundamental developmental task.

The term "deprivation" can refer to a lack of psychological stimulation and satisfaction as well. Psychological deprivation is not an easy term to define, although most clinicians have a sense of what the term means. One aspect of psychological deprivation has to do with the function adults serve as teachers, whose time and ministrations enable the child to grow and learn about the world. During the postnatal period all mammalian parents teach their offspring how to survive. Human caregivers spend considerable time responding to young children's biological— that is, physical and emotional— needs, ensuring their safety and teaching them about human relationships and the wider world. Through this process the child is civilized, that is, prepared to live in the social community of the next generation of adults.

For the developing human infant, psychological deprivation may be a much more serious issue than is commonly realized. Many studies, mostly in animals but also to a limited degree in human neurological development, suggest that infants need certain amounts of stimulation to organize and develop their central nervous system.

Relatively little is known about the biological processes that organize the brain, either before or after birth. We do know that this process of organization means that certain neuronal connections and pathways are strengthened while others are deemphasized. Use of certain pathways probably influences the development of new connections and the relative balance of connections that already exist.[3] This process probably unfolds in an orderly sequence, so that certain areas of the brain, and thus certain cognitive and psychological capabilities are vulnerable, or more vulnerable, to stimulation or damage at some times in development and not at others. These have been called "critical periods."

We suspect that parental failure to mediate external stimulation so it can mesh with the child's internal neuropsychological development and with the level and nature of stimulation the child can tolerate is likely to cause damage in two ways: it affects the brain's structural neuronal architecture, and it impedes the child's ability to progress to more advanced developmental capabilities. If this hypothesis is correct, the damage would make comprehensible the extraordinary difficulty clinicians experience in trying to reverse these deficits later in life.

In the developing infant, parental feeding and holding of the child are associated with the child's developing a psychological bond to the parent. In the last 40 years, developmental psychologists have realized that this bonding process in infancy has a profound effect on a person's ability to form subsequent relationships. Damage in this area may be hidden; only careful observation or psychological evaluation can determine it.[4] Because this damage is less obvious than bruises or broken bones, courts may consider it too subjective for intervention. In a previous paper,[5] we discussed how the judicial process might respond to this problem. Relatively little is known about assessing or quantifying such injury, yet those who see these children observe the damage to a child's potential for forming relationships too often for the observation to be ignored. Until further research, particularly longitudinal studies, help us define more precisely the impact that emotional abuse and neglect have, we must rely on the diagnostic techniques we now have at our disposal and on experienced professionals' judgment. Although the damage is subtle, it is substantial. These children have a great many difficulties with themselves, with other children, and with adults. Given their sense of extreme deprivation, they find it very difficult to share. Frequently they steal. Yet given their intense feelings of dissatisfaction with themselves, it is understandable that these children often find "not having" intolerable. For them to delay gratification is difficult, since it depends in part on confidence that the gratification indeed will appear in the future. Taking turns, which reflects children's willingness to submerge their own psychological needs for the group's welfare, may be too great a sacrifice. These children may seek companionship, but become extremely frustrated with what being part of a group requires and wind up antagonizing other children. Fighting or leaving the group is often the outcome.

Separation and Loss of Caring Figures

Many recent articles and books have described how disruptive and often destructive losing a parent, temporarily or permanently, is to a child. Maltreated children who end up being hospitalized or referred to residential treatment usually have experienced many disruptions in their lives and changes in their primary caregiver. They start out being deprived by their parents, but the system into which they are placed for protection is not designed to meet their most fundamental needs. They move back and forth among many family members, neighbors, babysitters, social workers, foster homes, and institutions.

In the 19th century it was said that all of medicine could be learned if one studied all aspects of syphilis. Today it might be said that the aberrations of the parent-child bond that are associated with mistreatment are, to a large degree, the core subject matter of psychodynamically oriented child psychiatry. Of particular concern in this context, however, is the question of dependency.

Many severely maltreated children display a degree of

pseudo-independence that leads them into conflict with the adult world. They are labeled as being resistive, oppositional, stubborn, difficult, and the like. If their traits were seen in a positive light some might be said to be "spunky," "feisty," "have a mind of their own," or be "a survivor." They show a strong ability not only to form their own views, but to persist in them no matter how unrealistic their perspective seems to adults. They might be called autonomous and self-reliant in a precocious fashion. Compared to normal children, they persist in trying to handle tasks beyond their capability rather than asking for help.

Although adults describe these traits as "willful" when mild or "oppositional" when severe, from the perspective of these children, this stance is entirely reasonable in light of their previous life experience. The toughness and independence these children exhibit has real survival value. It helps them to cope with the many unpredictable changes, disappointments, and fears that are a daily experience for them. Before coming into care, these children have had little opportunity to develop a sense of consistency or predictability in even the most simple activities or human relationships. They often cannot develop a sense that adults respond reliably; no one in their life has responded consistently. This difficulty shows up when the children are in care.

Because of a change in age mix of the children, hospital staff members attempted to rearrange the grouping in a rather hasty fashion. The children protested strongly. A 13-year-old girl, who had witnessed her mother kill her chronically violent father, yelled in great frustration, "I have been in seven different places in the last six months. I don't want any more moves." The staff wisely rescinded the change and made the girl a part of a group that would discuss any possible future rearrangements.

Typically, therapeutically oriented adults who deal with these children start out with a relatively benevolent perspective. However, the children see all adults as uncaring and unresponsive, no matter what evidence exists to the contrary. They fail to appreciate or value the adults' positive intentions. This rejection is likely to produce a disappointed if not also an angry response from the adults, who may have expected the waifs to appreciate some human kindness. The clinicians may feel that the children are ingrates who have spit upon their good intentions and may act in a rejecting or uncaring way, as a defensive response. Unfortunately for these children, this response confirms their previous view that the adult world is nasty and out to get them.

These children typically adopt a counterdependent stance and minimize the pain associated with psychological injury. They resemble small warriors— tough, denying pain, quick to fight, and always on guard against a cruel, cold world. Like the samurai, when injured they show their anger but not their hurt. On closer examination, their anxiety is apparent in nightmares, difficulty making simple decisions, nervous mannerisms, clinging to security objects, and low tolerance for ambiguous situations.

Under somewhat different circumstances, the same anger that is often expressed outwardly can be directed inwardly. In moments of frustration and self-hatred, these children can mutilate themselves or destroy their favored toys and other valued possessions. After all, tough guys don't need teddy bears, and anger must be discharged against something.

In contrast to these extremely independent children, another group is extraordinarily dependent and at first glance appear to cause society less trouble. These children cling to any adult they see as a potentially benevolent figure. They fail to discriminate well between strangers and well-known caregivers. Thus they may talk to people they encounter on the street with the same degree of familiarity they use with foster parents. They seem permanently fixed in this dependent stance. In contrast to more normal children who connect with an adult and then let go, caregivers describe these children as insatiable in their clinging. Some children in this group have excessive somatic preoccupations and rely on somatic complaints as a means of seeking nurturance and relief from anxiety. Although these children are easier to deal with on the surface, their passive reaction to their maltreatment may sacrifice a large potential inherent in their personality. Angry children maintain their sense of self— albeit as embattled soldiers surrounded by enemies, forced to defend body, honor, and soul— but many of the clingy children are simply broken, their will and sense of self diminished, if not destroyed.

Depression

Almost all of these severely mistreated children are deeply discouraged about themselves and the world.[6] Deep inside, they are extremely sad beings. They see themselves as worthless, which, given the way their parents and the world has treated them, is an understandable conclusion. They are the castoffs and throwaways. In one gang of such children, the symbol of membership was a tattooed tear below the eye.

Normal children internalize a sense that they are worthwhile and valuable through their satisfying relationship with adults. A good paradigm is the three-year-old who delights in showing off skills to the parent. "Come and see, daddy, see how high I can climb on the jungle gym!" Unspoken is, "Aren't I special and precious and wonderful?" When the parent smiles, the child takes the smile inside and carries the memory as part of their self-esteem. "I am the sort of person whose father smiles at them because they are so good."

In countless such experiences, which reflect the love and caring of the parent and the joy the parent experiences in the child, the child develops a sense of worth. Children who have not had these experiences constantly struggle with a sense that they are worthless. They do not have smiles to internalize and images of their goodness to carry inside. The self-respect that for many children develops from the good-enough relationship with one or both parents is missing. As one child put it, "I'm different from the other kids at my school. I'm a group home kid. We're second-rate."

In a fashion similar to other seriously emotionally disturbed children, these children often are distressed about their inability to control their behavior during an angry outburst, for they are aware of how their outbursts and tantrums antagonize important people in their life. Not infrequently, this distress turns into self-hatred and leads to self-mutilating behavior. Some of these children, as they grow older and progress to juvenile jails, have tattoos that say, "Born to Lose," or "Born to Die," not only accurately reflecting their self-view, but also advertising it in a desperate plea for help. The tattoo often reflects in a poignant way the parental wish that the children were dead, or the children's unconscious sense that the parent wanted to kill them.

In adapting to their chronic discouragement about life, many of these children develop a fatalistic view. How can those who are born to die put value on their own lives or the lives of others? As one child put it, "If I live, I live. If I die, I die. Who cares?"

Reality Distortion and Denial

Many parents who seriously maltreat their children force them to accept a subjective interpretation of situations that totally contradicts the child's direct experience. One night, the child might see his drunk father hit his mother. The next morning, if the child mentions the episode, the mother will say, "Nothing happened. Your dad didn't hit me. You're making it up." The father might deny that he had been drinking and react angrily to the child even raising the possibility that something unusual or upsetting might have happened the evening before. [7]

In similar fashion, some children whose fathers molest them, for example, attempt to tell their mothers. Some mothers respond, "Nothing is happening; don't you ever tell anyone such stories about your father again. If you tell such lies I'll spank you."

Denials of overt reality are extremely confusing and distressing. Children who believe the denials come to doubt their ability to observe reality accurately. Many wonder if they are insane; after all, they see and experience things that other people tell them are made up. The long-term impact is often that these children learn to operate in two realities; one that accepts the parental view, and the second, which the children keep hidden, that holds on to their own perceptions.

When the children start to reveal such secrets, this becomes an important issue. These children are unsure whether they will be believed, or whether the clinicians will repeat the message they received from their parents— these things didn't happen. If adults are willing to listen, acknowledge, and respect what the children say, this event marks a drastic change from their previous experience.

For the children we treat, the traumatic experiences did occur. Even if subjective perception has distorted the memories, they are neither psychological constructs nor fantasies. A clinician is well advised to respect what a child says unless there is good reason not to. In this therapeutic situation, which is quite different from that in which a clinician is doing an evaluation as an independent expert on behalf of the court, the clinician's responsibility is to the child. Children may be strengthened greatly if they are accepted, believed, and helped to realize how natural their emotions were in such unnatural circumstances. Validating their emotional reactions is important in helping children accept themselves and develop confidence in their own perceptions and judgment.

Disorganization

Many of these children have not experienced organized living. By "organized" we mean regularity in rhythm, regularity in space, and predictable causality. Organization and consistency are important because children tend to model their inner life and personality structure on the template the environment provides. External structure is a necessary condition for the child to develop internal structure. For these children, the tasks and rhythms of daily living often have not been reliable. When food is to be served, it may appear at six, eight, ten, or not at all. Bedtimes and awakenings are not repetitive in routine or in time. The family's possessions may be scattered about erratically. No adult consistently helps these children to organize their personal space and possessions. Thus, a four-year-old's clothes are not stored, beds are not made, toys are strewn here and there, and so forth.

Without external organization, these children do not develop internal organization over time and space. They fail to develop the sense of causality we see in more normal children— the sense that, "If I do A, then B will happen." Their disorganized world is unpredictable, focused on the immediate moment. "If Mom feels good, I'll eat. If she doesn't, I may not." In such a framework the mechanisms for learning to delay gratification do not occur, because the child cannot be confident that future gratification will take place in any predictable way. If food is available, gobble and hoard it, for who knows if tomorrow will bring famine and hunger.

The lack of external organization and predictability also makes it impossible for them to develop an internal sense of predictability— to use routine and order to master and control anxiety. Most children learn at an early age to use routine and ritual as a means of coping with the anxiety they feel when separated from their source of security, the parental figures. The lack of order in these children's lives prevents them from developing such techniques, and so they are often much more anxious than other children.

As a means of creating a more homelike environment, the clinicians in charge of a program once attempted to introduce a change in the way meals were served. They were surprised when the young children hesitated over accepting the change. Finally one of the children said, "But it's a change. I don't like things changing."

The high anxiety level of these children is frequently manifest in their very high activity level, and their inability to sit quietly in a peaceful or restful state. Constant activity wards off depressive, sad, or anxious feelings. As one 15-year-old girl, who had been a prostitute since age 11, put it, "I kept myself too busy to have time to feel scared." Because of this high activity level, these children may at times be misdiagnosed as suffering from a neurological deficit or an inherent Attention Deficit Disorder (ADHD), when the non-stop movement actually signifies their anxiety. Of course, ADHD may be part of the clinical constellation we describe.

Physical Attack

Recently, clinicians have been interested in the psychological effects of trauma. They have focused on overwhelming emotional experiences, whether they be combat, rape,[8] kidnapping,[9] or violence,[10] from a parent or some other person. Over time, normal children must develop mechanisms to cope with anxieties inherent in separating from parents and living in the world "out there." Based on a good-enough experience with parents, we construct the comforting illusion that we are secure as a way of making our lives easier. This illusion is not available to children whose parents beat them mercilessly. For them neither home nor the external world is perceived as safe. Fear, mistrust, and guardedness are not psychotic aberrations. They are the appropriate responses of intelligent people trying to understand their situations. One simply takes for granted the view that the world is a dangerous and unpredictable place if that has been one's experience. As one abused child, now grown up and in therapy, put it, "You call it paranoia, but I call it reasonable caution." In discussing her hospital experience, a teenager said, "I don't think I've ever felt safe before. It's so weird. It's so easy here because you know what's going to happen next, and they won't hit you or call you names if you make a mistake."

These children have felt helpless and frightened when they were attacked. These feelings are enduring, powerful influences that appear in play, dreams, and associations. They may come up in unpredictable situations. Even remembering such past experiences can be distressing, and until they are ready, children typically strongly prefer not to think or talk about such experiences. Suddenly recalling a painful episode may cause a child to experience acute distress, a feeling translated rapidly into disruptive behavior.

Naive or inexperienced therapists may fail to recognize or respect the intense emotional upset caused by traumatic episodes, and thus may not respect the fragile defenses these children have constructed to contain the overwhelming feelings these abusive, humiliating experiences have produced. Out of a sincere but misguided desire to help a child, a clinician may force a child to remember, think about, describe, and even emotionally relive traumatic events. For some children this is profoundly disturbing, which is why they typically try to avoid it. Often the child may gradually "forget" the specific experience, while still retaining the behavioral and emotional sequelae related to it that appear in play.[11]

If children are forced to recall the trauma, they may become acutely anxious, guilty, depressed, or enraged. The overwhelming emotions the painful memories evoke may compromise their emotional stability and cause them to lose control over their behavior. Both the children and the caregivers faced with the difficult job of restoring stability are likely to see the resulting explosion or episode of self-mutilation negatively.

A 13-year-old girl began telling her therapist about when she was five. Her father had placed his penis in her mouth, which gagged her. Following the session she had nightmares for the next three nights. No intervention calmed her. The therapist wisely suggested that such thoughts might be so upsetting that for the time being, it might be more constructive to spend time thinking about ways she might feel safer and better in the present.

Many of these children think of themselves not as "abused" but as "bad" children. Through their misbehavior, they have antagonized their parents and thus provoked punishment they deserve. They may be embarrassed to talk about having been punished, in part because these children often view the punishment as legitimate. In their minds, the discussion is a revelation of how they misbehaved and why they deserved mistreatment. Only over time, as they feel safe, can these children start to review past events in a more thoughtful, less charged way.

For most of these children, danger has not been a single event but a continuing process. So how do they deal with persistent threats to their well-being? In our experience, they react in several ways when they are threatened.

One strategy they use is to try to pacify the potentially dangerous figure. In our view all children are to some degree scared of their parents, who are, after all, so much bigger and stronger, and whose love and attention the children need so badly. The desire to please parents is part of both every child's love for the parent and their reaction to anxiety born of fear. In the abusive situation, in deference to a threatening parent, children may subjugate themselves even more extremely. These abused children are excessively compliant, and concentrate on placating adults. They are extremely anxious and guilt ridden, and often develop a self-deprecating style. They accept the aggressive adult's view that they are bad. These children are passive and dependent, and see themselves as servile; their major goal in life is gratifying others.

Girls with this perspective who have been sexually abused frequently become promiscuous or prostitutes. They have accepted a negative view of themselves that the maltreating parents have inculcated; they perpetuate this relationship with the new man who "loves and needs" them. Thus a relationship with a pimp may have strong elements that repetitively recreate this theme. A teenage prostitute described her relationship with her abusive boyfriend: "I'm a bad little girl at heart. I need a strong man to protect me and keep me in line when I'm naughty. My whole life is keeping him happy."

Sometimes children who start out in this pattern later switch to a more resistant, rebellious mode. One child described this change as occurring when "I realized that I didn't have to take being beaten any more. I could fight back." Although this realization represents a healthier response, it can lead children into more conflict with the adult world. A timid, withdrawn, compliant child becomes angry, rebellious, and challenging in school. Although we might consider it a therapeutic milestone, the child's teacher will not usually be pleased. Physically resisting or striking back against parents may also cause a crisis in the home, with a marked increase in the level of destructive behavior on the part of both parent and child. At this point the child may come to the attention of mental health or social services, accused of being an evil or bad child who has struck a parent. What may not be presented is the previous history that has led to this "slave's revolt." Occasionally such situations lead to a child killing a parent, or vice versa, although more typically the child leaves or runs away from the home as a means of avoiding further violence.

Many children respond to the parent hitting them with great outrage, bitterness, and a deep sense that they have been violated. Their anger often is displaced outside the home on secondary authority figures such as teachers, other children, or animals, or in destructiveness to property. Occasionally children torture animals in a fashion similar to their home experience. One child whose father sodomized him stuck a pencil up his pet guinea pig's anus and killed it.[12] Firesetting and other forms of destructive vandalism frequently may represent the intense anger such children feel toward the world.

Often these children are especially uncomfortable about physical contact. In reaction to sudden adult moves, they may flinch or attack defensively, particularly if the adult is seen in some way as threatening. An adult using gentle physical contact, such as taking a child's hand to guide or steer the child, may find the maneuver having the unexpected effect of antagonizing the child or evoking a hostile, even violent reflexive response.

Sexual Activity

Many of these children have been exposed to, or involved in, sexual activities at a very young age. Often, the adult involved is a family member. To understand the effect these sexual activities have on children, we must acknowledge that these activities vary in their nature and that the significance and meaning children ascribe to them is not uniform. The way the activity was initiated; the age of the child at the time when it started; its frequency; the degree to which it was psychologically consensual (since these children are all too young to truly give consent, we use this term to mean those who are seduced and enticed rather than being threatened, coerced, or brutally forced); the techniques the molester used to keep the activity a secret; what the child's relationships with other adults were like; the nature of the family system and the way in which the family and society reacted when the activity was revealed—all affect how a child understands what happened.[13] The oversimplifying term "sexual abuse" does not do justice to this complexity. Consider the following somewhat arbitrarily defined groups.

For some children, sexual activity was a coercive, painful event devoid of physical pleasure, and suffered under duress to avoid having more severe physical pain inflicted on them or to avoid death, or to preserve the family's stability. For this group, fear, power, and domination are major themes. These children's adaptations may be interwoven with simply trying to survive when their home environment is very dangerous. In these cases, the sexual activity has an impact that is similar to the impact rape has on adults, where fear and coercion play such an important role. The main difference is that ordinarily we think of rape as a single event, whereas in relation to children the pattern may be repeated many times over many years.

For other children, the sexual activity, although abusive, may have been more like an adult romantic affair in tone. The sexual activity may be introduced slowly, with gradual increments in seriousness. Some children may have found it physically pleasurable, at least at times. Furthermore, children who have been neglected in the past may have been given extra privileges as a reward for participating in this "special" relationship with the adult. When the relationship is terminated, these children may feel that they have lost something valuable, as well as enormous confusion and betrayal. Occasionally the sexual activity with the adult is highly pleasurable physically and psychologically; in fact it may be the only source of pleasure the children experience. Some children may become highly erotic, and unable to differentiate sensual from affectionate touch.[14] They may never learn to sublimate their sexual drives or to form nonerotic relationships; they tend to repeat this pattern with multiple adults.

A somewhat different group consists of children who have witnessed a great deal of adult sexual activity either directly or in magazines and films. This leaves them preoccupied with sexual themes in their language and play. Still another group may use sexual language or behavior in a provocative, hostile way because they have found it to be a powerful tool.

These experiences are obviously different, and the psychological issues each child faces reflect those differences.

Fairness

Children who resist the perspective that they deserve mistreatment often feel that the world has treated them unfairly. Although in middle and late childhood most children suffer from the understandable "delusion" that the world is actually a fair place where right always prevails over might, for these mistreated children the sense of being unfairly treated is particularly strong. Incidental living situations that in some way provoke or intensify the feeling that they are being treated unfairly are likely to produce strong resentment. Punishment, and particularly punishment that children perceive as being undeserved, often evokes intense rage and destructiveness. For these children such situations are yet another incident where they are victims of injustice, which leads them to vent the rage they feel toward the many previous injustices in their lives.

Those who are living with these children thus face a difficult clinical situation. First, the dynamics of the ward or cottage as a group at times may force the adults to ignore an individual child's best interests and to take some sort of preemptive negative action against one child so that other children in the group do not exact personal revenge. Second, the staff may hold to very different standards and values from the child regarding what constitutes appropriate behavior and what justifies punishment. An obvious example is one child's hitting another. The child who was hit is likely to consider counterattack as the appropriate response— if hit, hit back— and the adult may need to act against the attacker to prevent open combat. Both children, however, may consider staff disapproval of their fighting as nonsensical and strongly oppose any punitive sanction.

From the child's perspective, if the figure causing the

injustice is an adult, the situation is even worse. A child from a better home situation might appeal to the other parent or be able to wait out the situation and then appeal to the offending parent when he or she is calmer. But children in care have so little faith in the good intentions of adults that such a course is not even part of their thinking. The idea that an adult might admit error or be responsive to appeal is contrary to their experience. Instead, they are likely to resort to some destructive act to protest the unfairness. Of course, the destructive act is likely to make the adult even more punitive, escalating the conflict. From the child's point of view, the adult's unfairness has caused the difficulty; from the adult's perspective, the child's reluctance to accept what the adult considers appropriate rules and necessary guidance forced the adult to respond lest the situation escalate out of control.

The peer group also has difficulty with this problem. If the clinician is not sufficiently punitive, the other children are confused. Even if the staff member compensates in some way (either materially or psychologically) for damage done to the group or to the other children, the psychological issues remain. The other children are likely to see the staff member as weak for failing to punish. Because of their previous experiences, some children will find the physical fighting very distressing and will worry about their own safety as well as the safety of their possessions. However, these episodes can be used to good therapeutic advantage. They may lead to a deeper discussion about punishment and its impact. But there is a hazard. Since many children in these settings rely on adult strictures as a source of control over their internal chaos, nonpunitive approaches can weaken tenuous controls for some group members.

Of course, even if these children are aware that they have transgressed group rules, they are likely to be reluctant to admit it. Since they have been lied to often, they see little value in honesty; second, in the past, admitting guilt was likely to lead to physical attack, third, admitting guilt may lead to a flood of self-deprecating feelings and a catastrophic loss of any sense of self-worth.

Destruction and Sadistic Feelings

The act of destruction gratifies some children. They are not alone. Many people experience this pleasure, albeit less intensely and in more controlled circumstances (as reflected by the pleasure people derive from demolition derbies at carnivals and car crashes on television). But why is this act satisfying? Certainly the pleasure associated with getting revenge is part of this process, but what makes revenge such a deep-seated and pleasurable human act?

Revenge is the desire to make other persons suffer in exchange or compensation for the suffering they have caused us. An eye for an eye, a tooth for a tooth, was the ancient rule. Revenge is an effort to restore power to the victim and to compensate for a feeling of powerlessness the injury caused. The goal is to reaffirm our power by humiliating or injuring someone who previously made us feel weak and helpless. Revenge is an effort toward psychological mastery of the experience of having been victimized.

Revenge is usually focused precisely. A boy entered a staff room and deliberately broke a child care worker's guitar, but left other persons' possessions undisturbed. Of course the boy was angry at that worker and wanted to retaliate against the worker's most precious posession. He thought that was the way to hurt the worker as deeply and personally as he had been hurt.

Even in the absence of overt, focused anger, destruction can be pleasurable. Breaking things provides a sense of power, a sense of being the boss rather than being bossed, of strength over the environment. The anger may be driven more by the children's world view than by a current situation.

By provoking and retaliating against a current wrong, children may relieve inner tension about past injustices. Their aggressive urges create anxiety in adults unless they are expressed in clearly circumscribed settings. Allowing children to give vent to their aggressiveness runs the hazard of contagion effects, with other children indulging these feelings, leading to a generalized loss of control. Also, destructiveness tends to offend the sense of thrift, control, and order that adults have— even if the objects that are broken have no useful value.

Although teaching children what should or shouldn't be destroyed is likely to be a much easier task than expecting them to contain these impulses completely, very few treatment programs provide opportunities for such destruction.

Destruction also provokes anxiety because it reminds us that we retain childhood urges to destroy, which we have more or less set aside as part of the price we pay to grow up. Like the alcoholic who cannot tolerate even one drink, some people are uncomfortable with even small amounts of aggressive destruction because they sense within themselves the need for strong controls over their own aggressive and destructive impulses.

Summary

Part three of this monograph has focused on the nature of the extreme mistreatment these children have received before coming into treatment, and how it has affected their world view. Because human relationships have been so inconsistent, dangerous, and unrewarding for them, these children enter the treatment situation with a perspective far different from the world view most of us have. Their unique upbringing and the anxiety we feel as we become aware that they have been severely traumatized make the treatment task difficult.

NOTES

1 Recent research suggests, at least in rats, tactile stimulation is essential for the production of growth hormone. See *Science* 239: 142.

2 Erickson, Eric, *Childhood and Society* (New York: Norton, 1950).

3 Aoki, C., and Siekevitz, P., "Plasticity in Brain Development," *Scientific American* (December 1988): 56–64.

4 See the original studies of Anna Freud and John Bowlby, and the more recent work by Ainsworth.

5 Wasserman, S., and Rosenfeld, A., "Decision Making in Child Abuse and Neglect," *Bulletin of the American Academy of Psychiatry Law* 13, 3 (1985).

6 A straightforward research study examining the prevalence of depression in children in residential care is presented in "The Prevalence of Adolescent Depression in a Residential Treatment Home Program," *Residential Treatment* 5, 3 (Spring 1988).

7 In this regard, see Cermak, T. A., *Time to Heal* (New York: Tarcher, St. Martin's Press, 1988).

8 Rose, D., "Worse Than Death—Psychodynamics of Rape Victims and the Need for Psychotherapy," *American Journal of Psychiatry* 143, 7 (July 1986): 817–824.

9 Terr, L. "Chowchilla Revisited: The Effects of Psychic Trauma Four Years after a School Bus Kidnapping," *American Journal of Psychiatry* 140 (1983a): 1543–1550.

10 _____. "What Happens to Early Memories of Trauma? A Study of Twenty Children," *Journal of the American Academy of Child and Adolescent Psychiatry* 27, 1 (1987): 96–104.

11 *Ibid.*

12 In 1750 William Hogarth did a series of etchings entitled "The Stages of Cruelty." In the first of the prints, a parish child (the equivalent of a contemporary child under the care of the state)

is inserting an arrow in the anus of a dog. The boy ultimately becomes a murderer.

13 Zivney, O.; Nash, M.; and Hulsey, T., "Sexual Abuse in Early Versus Late Childhood: Differing Patterns of Pathology as Revealed on the Rorschach," *Psychotherapy* 25, 1 (Spring 1988); Nash, M.; Zivney, O.; and Hulsey, T., "Types of Sexual Abuse Associated with Greater Psychological Impairment Among Children," *Victimology* (in review).

14 Yates, A., "Children Eroticized by Incest," *American Journal of Psychiatry* 139 (1982): 482–486.

IV

Aspects of Treatment

In part three, we discussed the nature of mistreated children's life experience, and how mistreatment affects a child's world view. We can now develop and implement treatment strategies that attempt to restore the child to a more healthy and satisfying emotional development. Part four discusses issues that frequently appear in the early phases of the treatment, complications and difficulties in treatment that the child's past has created, feelings that treating these children arouse in staff and therapist, some goals, and a method of achieving certain goals.

No treatment can obliterate the memory of overwhelmingly bad experiences; nor can therapy make the emotional impact of those experiences go away entirely. If a girl remembers a parent raping her and trying to choke her to death, therapy cannot "reframe" that experience so that she sees it as cheery, pleasant, or even neutral. Treatment may change her understanding of why the experience occurred. By giving her rewarding experiences and a sense of security in human relationships, a corrective life experience that when placed in the balance allows her to feel that overall, life is more than a hopeless endeavor or a series of horrible experiences, treatment can prevent these experiences from entirely dominating her world view. For these grossly maltreated children, who feel themselves to be very different from others, who feel themselves to be outsiders, monsters, animals, and rejects, treatment can help them develop the belief that they can be understood, accepted, and that even for them life can be somewhat nourishing and worthwhile. That hope and that world view allow them to build a better life for themselves.

Although these principles appear almost self-evident, translating them into action is far from simple.

Perspective on the Mistreatment

Therapy can influence children's perceptions of why they were maltreated, thereby changing its psychological impact. Many abused children believe that the harsh parental treatment they received was entirely their fault. Maltreating parents typically blame the children not only for their misbehavior, but for all family and marital difficulties. The children are told repeatedly that their misconduct justifies the maltreatment or excessive violence in discipline. To the children, parents are larger, superior in intellect and skills. Children do not understand cause and effect the way adults do, and are physically and psychologically dependent on parents. Therefore, they almost always accept the parents' explanation for the events, and concur with the adults' view that the family's problems are entirely the children's fault.

For example, an uncle molested his eight-year-old niece and then beat her as punishment. As far as the girl, now a psychiatric patient, has been able to reconstruct the experience, her "crime" was being in the home alone with the uncle and thus drawing attention to herself. Her uncle told her that the molestation was her fault and that she deserved the punishment she was then given for what *she* had done. Since she didn't understand what she had done she concluded that her offense was related to some inherent quality in her that aroused sexual impulses in her uncle. From that point on she considered herself a bad figure who corrupted men. Being raped while a teenager confirmed this view. She often contemplated suicide, which she saw as an altruistic act that would eliminate from the earth the curse that she carried.

In an effort to master the trauma and to make it understandable, to comprehend why the painful events occurred, children create a subjective explanation. The belief that they caused the trauma can give the children the illusion that they control a situation that made them feel helpless and overwhelmed. The attempt is constructive in that its aim is to detoxify the experience, making it less frightening and confusing. That would make the child feel stronger and in more control. Perhaps the child who was raped teased the parent beforehand, had angry feelings toward the mother, or was showing off. In a psychological sense, blaming oneself is actually less frightening than blaming the parent, who is the child's whole world. "If I have caused my misery, I can behave better and prevent its recurrence. Thinking this way, I retain a sense of control over my destiny." Unfortunately, the mechanism of self-blame also damages the child's self-respect and sense of worth. Psychotherapy allows a child to sort out feelings and experiences into their component parts and to reexamine them in a new light. Thus it helps the child distinguish which aspects of the abusive experience, if any, they contributed to and which were entirely the adult's responsibility.

A ten-year-old girl had recently seen her father murder her mother. The police and attorneys interviewed her extensively, but no one paid much attention to her needs or feelings about what she had seen. When she entered therapy and began to explore her recollections in detail, she was relieved to conclude that nothing she could have done that day would have averted the tragedy. Her sense of guilt did not dissipate entirely. She retained doubts about whether if she had behaved better while she was growing up in the family, her mother might still be alive.

A 30-year-old woman who had been an incest victim complained repeatedly to her therapist about a supervisor who she felt was maltreating her. She saw this supervisor as a "maniac" who was beyond reasonable discussion. As a consequence of treatment she confronted her supervisor, who was first surprised, but considered the woman's complaint, decided she was right, and corrected the problem.

This response shocked the patient, because she realized that through suffering silently she had allowed herself to remain in a victim role. For a long time after this episode the patient examined her propensity to divide people into victims and victimizers. With further long-term therapy and a mature adult's perspective she decided that seeing the issue in terms of villains and victims weakened her, for she tended to see herself as a potential victim of villains in other situations. That expectation empowered the others and left her depleted. To repossess her power she insisted that she would not allow herself to be treated abusively again, that she would no longer be the receptacle for other persons' destructive psychological needs and problems. Most importantly, she realized that both she and the other people in the world could have a more respectful, satisfying relationship, for if she were not a helpless victim, the others were not necessarily rapacious monsters. When she stopped seeing people as victimizers, she was rejected less often.

A stepfather repeatedly molested his adolescent stepdaughter. He threatened that if she did not comply with his sexual demands he would beat both her and her mother. Ultimately this girl attempted, and almost committed, suicide, and was admitted to a psychiatric ward. At first she condemned herself mercilessly. As therapy progressed, however, she gradually became angry at her stepfather, and less angry at herself. Her mood improved and her suicidal feelings disappeared. After extensive discussions with her therapist, she decided to bring criminal charges against her stepfather. When the police investigated, they found that he had twice previously married women with young daughters and then molested the children.

Change in World View

Treating these children probably differs most from more traditional therapy in that clinicians must make intense efforts to change the children's fundamental world view. As indicated previously, these children see adults, authority, themselves, and life negatively. This world view leads them into self-defeating behavior and creates a self-perpetuating situation. A neurotic person has internalized positive authority figures, usually the early childhood relationship with a parent. The therapist can draw on these internalized images to form a positive relationship with the patient. Severely mistreated children have had very few constructive relationships, so the clinician must continuously demonstrate that a relationship with an adult can have positive elements.

How does the adult clinician go about changing an abused child's view of adults? We might say that since these children have lived through a very bad experience, they need to live through a good experience to begin healing. The task is long and arduous, but starts with a simple principle. By being child focused, by being responsive to the children's needs as they define them, and by being concerned about the child's feelings, the clinician presents the children with an experience different from the ones they have known previously. The children need to have a corrective life experience, analogous to the corrective emotional experience of traditional therapy. As the children go through the corrective experience, they begin to incorporate the feelings, views, and attitudes they have experienced with positive adult authority figures and use them to counterbalance the negative previous experiences. Since the child care staff members are the new parent figures, they and not the individual therapist must provide most of this corrective life experience. Although this sounds simple in concept, forces within the children, forces within the treating caregivers, and forces within the institution make the process formidable.

The Negative World View—The Negative Transference

The clinicians must proceed to modify the child's view that all human relationships are painful and abusive. This task may be difficult to conceptualize, since on the face of it, the adults must live with aggressive, destructive, explosive, hateful children. Because these children have had such negative experiences, often with violent adults, they naturally assume that interactions with adults at the treatment facility will also be abusive and destructive. They approach adults with fear, anxiety, guilt, anger and a propensity to avoid relationships. This can annoy the adults, who sense the child's distance and sense that the child acts as if they were abusive adults. By holding adults in such low esteem, the children may, in effect, insult them and thereby trigger vindictive responses. The children's suspiciousness, mistrust, and lack of respect for adults may lead them to provoke and frustrate the clinicians, increasing the likelihood that staff members will retaliate in ways that confirm the children's expectations. This can initiate and sustain the cycle we have outlined previously of increasing mutual anger between adults and children.

Children have been placed in a restrictive setting because they are so disturbed that their behavior has become a serious problem. No one likes destructive outbursts. The question the clinicians face is, "What therapeutic interventions will decrease the children's destructiveness in the long run?" The internal state that led to the destructive behavior and the fear and mistrust of adults that make a child destructive are much harder to understand and accept than observing that a child has smashed a window.

The child breaking the window makes us angry, and in our anger we are vulnerable to losing the opportunity to learn something that might be useful, both to the child and to us, something that might prevent such behavior in the future. The danger of approaching a child who has smashed a window (or has done some other destructive act) simply from a perspective that tries to extinguish antisocial behavior is that it fails to consider set, setting, and motivation from the child's perspective. A clinical approach that deals only with overt behavior can rapidly be used to justify punitive responses; these responses contribute further to the child's pessimistic feeling that the world only misunderstands and punishes him. If the child is a delinquent boy trying to prove his masculinity, such an approach may provoke a struggle to prove who is more powerful and lead to more aggressive behavior. In the long run, punitive approaches are nonproductive because they do little to alter the child's world view, which is what led to the destructive behavior in the first place. In the short run, such approaches may actually increase the probability of more window smashing and lead to the child being transferred to a more restrictive environment because he or she is unmanageable.

If the clinicians take the time to sincerely ask the child, "What made you so angry?" or even better, "What did we do to make you so angry?" it is amazing to see that children who previously have been described as unthinking and inarticulate often can define precisely what made them so frustrated. The child's perspective must be heard and acknowledged first. Once children feel listened to, and become aware that the adults respond to their loss of control with interest and not with rage, the children and adults can make sense of the episode, figuring out what would be an appropriate immediate response and what staff and child can do to prevent outbursts in the future. Such an experience may lead children to value the treatment setting more. Some become willing to behave better to preserve the adults' good opinion of them. The key is that during a tense period, adults respond in a way that surprises the children and moves them out of their defensive stance. This process can help promote growth and correct the distortions that led to the outburst.

Destructive behavior signifies that something is not going well for the child and should never be ignored. The situation requires serious attention to prevent more destructiveness.

An eight-year-old girl started banging loudly on the unit door, disrupting everyone. Ultimately she had to be secluded. When queried, she pointed out that her therapist had failed to tell her clearly whether or not her drug-using mother would be allowed to visit that week. (Her mother was allowed to visit only if her urine was free of drugs at her drug treatment program.) The girl was correct; the therapist had been preoccupied and had neglected what the girl considered crucial. He agreed to attend to it quickly. The therapist also pointed out that he would have responded to the girl if she had simply told him she was concerned. They agreed that banging on doors was not the most constructive way to be heard. The girl went back to class.

Stealing is another common symptom that illustrates the therapeutic issue. One way to approach the behavior is from a moral perspective, condemning it as wrong and punishing it. Of course it is wrong, despite the fact that very few adults will maintain that they have not stolen things as children. But if one is concerned primarily with therapeutic growth rather than morality, stealing can be viewed primarily as a sign that the child is angry over deprivation, as reflecting a child's sense of having been wronged and not given to in the past. Stealing is not usually random; staff members can learn a great deal by carefully observing exactly what has been stolen. This observation can be used creatively in treatment.

A 13-year-old girl had been arrested for shoplifting beef jerky while a runaway and was taken to a juvenile jail. She then was transferred to a treatment program. She had been in conflict with her mother for a long time and then ran away; in reality she had felt uncared for since her grandmother had died of cancer four years previously. Her grandmother had been the person who had raised the child. The therapist arranged to have beef jerky in his office, so the girl "would not have to get into trouble to get something she needed so much." Ultimately the girl formed a strong positive relationship with the therapist and the program, and started to sort out her feelings about losing her grandmother and having a bad relationship with her mother.

An explosive 17-year-old boy told how his father would not let him have both pizza and a cola at the same meal. According to the father, having two fun things at one meal was wrong and would not be tolerated. The child care staff members indicated their willingness to eliminate such unnecessary dietary frustrations and thereby helped defuse his anger and distance themselves from the punitive parent.

Punishing or depriving abused or neglected children as part of a treatment strategy is dangerous in other ways. If the children believe that the punishment is warranted, and we have stimulated their pervasive sense of worthlessness, they are likely to become more guilty and depressed. Since many of these children already struggle with intense self-hatred, the punishment may lead to self-mutilating or suicidal behavior; if the inner tension becomes unbearable, children may externalize the feelings and become assaultive, certainly an undesirable outcome.

An eight-year-old boy refused to go to school and was made to sit on the floor outside the classroom. He began banging his head against the wall. When the staff reviewed the situation with him he revealed that he had been severely beaten at home for poor school performance and felt very bad about his difficulties in school. Once the teacher understood his problem, she devised a "guaranteed success" program whose aim was simply to make him feel more comfortable in the classroom.

Even if the children do not resist overtly, unfair punishment almost inevitably damages the positive relationships the clinicians have worked so hard to build. If the children feel that they do not deserve the punishment, they may acquiesce, but they will carry inside strong internal resentment about being treated unfairly. The experience will corroborate their conviction that the world (and the program) is as cold and insensitive as they had previously believed it to be. They already harbor strong feelings of having been unfairly treated. If the children do resist, the adults are likely to respond with more forceful coercion and more punitive responses. This creates a power struggle that is likely to be psychologically destructive and will most certainly interfere with the adults and children living together comfortably.

A night shift worker told a teenage girl that because she had been noisy and disruptive at night, she could not smoke the next day. Since the girl was addicted to cigarettes, she threatened to run away. In the morning she did. After she had "bummed a smoke" she came back. She might have been punished further to set limits on her behavior. But several staff members who smoked pointed out that the punishment had been severe. These staff members spoke to the girl and found out that she was having recurrent nightmares about a previous molestation. In response to these bad dreams she awoke during the night feeling very bad and had ruminative thoughts about hurting herself. She needed a cigarette to calm down. Although they knew that it would create issues that would need to be worked out at a staff meeting because of the night staff person's resentment about not being supported, they decided to take a different tack. Once the night staff member heard about the girl's bad dreams, she was more sympathetic. The group decided that a child care worker the girl especially liked would give her hot soup and extra TLC at bedtime. The girl was encouraged to spend the twilight time thinking about something good that had happened to her that day, or to plan something positive for the next day. The night staff workers told the girl that when she was upset at night she should try to let them know, and they would try respond in a more supportive and helpful way. This arrangement worked well. Eventually this girl was able to sleep through the night without incident.

Traumatic experiences may leave unusual symptoms behind as sequelae. The connection between the symptom and the event may be suppressed, although the impact and effect remain. Much behavior that seems quirky or idiosyncratic is the direct result of the child's experience.[1] For example, a ten-year-old boy disliked riding in vans. During the course of a conversation, the boy became very upset when the recollection flashed through his mind: his stepmother had forced him to engage in cunnilingus with her in a van. Two years after this conversation he still disliked riding in vans but had no idea why he felt that way.

Early-Phase Treatment Goals

To work successfully with these children the therapist needs to be clear about treatment goals, and to develop a sense of priorities. Adults who are used to dealing with children with less severe problems, or adults who rely solely on their personal life experience and upbringing, may seriously underestimate severely mistreated children's disturbance. This misassessment often is based on the child's normal or appealing physical appearance, or the child's self-control during periods that are not stressful. It can lead adults to establish goals or to have expectations that are unrealistic. When the children fail to meet these goals, the adults may get angry and discouraged. Out of disappointment, doubts surface about the children's treatability, and staff members drift toward using more punitive measures. Both the children's and clinicians' morale can deteriorate.

In our experience, the safest (and most realistic) course of action is to presume that the children are doing the best they can under the circumstances, and to focus on achieving the most basic goal—living together as comfortably as possible. The staff ought to aim to get through each block of time, each shift or each day perhaps, in a way that leaves the children and the caregiving adults feeling good about the day and about their experience together. Although this goal seems minimal, in practical terms it is quite ambitious with children who have had so few days that have not been filled with tension and upheaval.

In their enthusiasm to help the children, clinicians frequently feel a strong desire to make the children ready to face the world. As laudable as this goal is in the long term, getting the children ready for the world involves remaking their picture of it; that is more likely to take years, not weeks or months. To act as if the children's situations can change quickly and forever is to try to wish away the children's life experiences and the pathology they have created. On short-term units, the clinicians may feel a sense of urgency based on the pressure of utilization review; even today's longer-stay residential facilities are often forced to prepare for the children's discharge before they can really get to know them. This can make the program focus on practical placement issues while ignoring the child's inner life. In this environment, where pressures from the state and other funding sources abound, clinicians can easily forget that learning occurs through small incremental steps, they can easily become frustrated and angry that progress is slow. The children sense this anger immediately, and are likely to feel guilty and to react defensively. When the going gets rough, the children may perceive the clinicians' mood accurately and suggest that the adults are trying to get rid of them. Even this can be productive if the children and adults explore why this rejecting situation came about in the face of the overall goal of simply living together comfortably from day to day.

Each good day gratifies both the children and the adults. By sharing in this pleasure, change begins. In a program that adheres to this philosophy it is not unusual to hear children say, "This is the first time I ever did well." Since they have failed so often and have such a strong sense that they are failures, this success gives them hope. It promotes the desire, both from adults and children, to continue the process, and starts to build a legacy of positives— accumulated assets of mutual good will.

An attractive, extremely aggressive seven-year-old was in a pleasant mood. Lost in enjoyable thoughts, he walked right past the cart to which he wanted to return his lunch tray. When he realized his mistake, he exclaimed, matter-of-factly, "Oh, shit!" and returned to the cart, where he stored his tray. His strong language distressed a visitor to the unit; such words ought not come from such a cherub. The program director could have easily felt annoyed at this child, who had embarrassed him in front of an important guest. Yet he knew the cherub's explosive capabilities, and was pleased that the child had used verbal means of dealing with his frustration rather than throwing the tray across the room. He did not interfere with the boy's good mood, and later explained his thinking to the guest.

The Need To Supply Direct Gratification

For these children to get through the day relatively comfortably, the adults must gratify them much more directly than children are typically gratified. At the start of treatment, more normal children have had some history of positive relationships, which enables them to accept fairly rapidly that the therapist has some positive aspects . In effect, the therapist draws on what was positive in the children's past relationships to build a therapeutic alliance. The therapist anticipates that this will lead to a healing relationship over time.

Children do not carry within themselves the concept that authority can be constructive unless they have once experienced it. Children with a previous poor experience can only fantasize about good relationships, and imagine them as ideal or total involvements that are all-gratifying and never frustrating. They exist somewhere "over the rainbow." The dream is that the adults will be all-knowing, all-satisfying, and always available. Unfortunately, such an ideal can never be achieved in real life. These severely mistreated children have little sense that actual adults, despite their limitations, can be interested, understanding, and responsive; as we have indicated previously, their view of adults is very much the opposite. Clinicians who hope to build a positive alliance with the children must first counteract the children's view that real adults are destructive and their idealized view of how adults ought to be. To initiate this process, the clinicians must provide positive experiences. This can be done in many ways, depending on the particular child. The clinicians aim to gratify the child in some unique way that appeals to the particular child. The goal, however, is not to simply gratify, but to respond in a way that has special meaning, that conveys the message that the child has been listened to carefully, and that his or her desires have been taken seriously.

One surprisingly simple way to start is to see if the child can remember any positive interaction with an adult in the past. The clinician tries to understand what the child found gratifying about that experience, and then recreates a similar situation. A child who had multiple parent figures reject her described the fun she had had when her father's girlfriend would take her out for exploratory walks and lunch. She enjoyed the friendly adult interest. Using this as a guide, the clinician initiated walks with stops at a local fast-food restaurant. The girl rapidly took to the clinician and the treatment went well.

Another child recounted how, when she was upset, her grandmother would take her out for ice cream and talks. Her treatment plan and the kitchen supplies were modified so that staff members could do the same. Although the girl had run away from other programs, she proudly announced later that she would not run away from this program because the people were "different, they were real friends." Had the girl said that her grandmother had bought her favorite flavor, "Rocky Road," "strawberry" might not have been adequate, for the goal was to treat *her* wishes as unique and valid.

The early phase of treating children who have had terrible life experiences is based on providing positive experiences that at least in symbolic form can serve as an antidote for the trauma they have experienced. As one boy put it, "You need ten good experiences to make up for one horrible one."

Some programs discount these concrete needs, considering them trivial, since these children have massive psychological needs. One program dismissed the children's complaint that they could not buy decent clothes on $50 every three months. After all, the program administrators reasoned, what needed remedy was the children's low self-esteem. Yet, can self-esteem be improved when a child must dress shabbily in comparison to other children in the community? We think not. Furthermore, we think that buying children nice clothing is a concrete demonstration that the program is concerned about their appearance. This heads the therapeutic process in the proper direction; it lets the children know that the therapeutic team believes that they can go from being and looking like throwaways to becoming fine, valuable human beings.

The Importance of Food and Feeding

Since these children often have a strong sense that they have been deprived, they need to be nurtured. The term "deprivation," as used here, goes beyond a sense of not having things other children have. The inner pessimism of these children is profound. They believe, "Because you have no worth, you cannot get anything you want or have anything go well." To make contact with their hope that somewhere, somehow, life can improve, the clinicians must first supply food for their hunger. With time, the adults help the child link the satisfaction food gives with the caring adults who provide it. Normal children make this linkage in infancy. Once deprived children make the linkage, the clinicians use that model of caring as the foundation on which positive human relationships can be built.

An 11-year-old girl had been removed from her home along with two younger siblings when she was three. Over the subsequent eight years she spent time in four foster homes.

Two siblings were adopted, but she was rejected. When she was admitted to a program, she was intensely stubborn and would attach to no one. Her only interest was in getting material things, particularly candy. Since she was quite discouraged about herself and the world, she found getting up in the morning difficult. "Why should I get up?" she asked her therapist, "I have nothing to look forward to." Finally, to encourage her, the clinician provided a roll of Lifesaver candy every morning as an incentive for her to rise.

One day, after several months of special treats, the girl asked the therapist for a bag of candy, which she explained she no longer wanted for herself. She had concluded that to make friends she should give candy to the other girls, as the therapist had done with her. Although the therapist had doubts and voiced them, they agreed to try it as an experiment. They were both delighted when it proved a useful and successful tool. The girl felt that she had received enough so that she was now able to share. No doubt the other children sensed that her stance had changed and were more willing to accept her candy, since she was no longer so self-centered. As the children accepted her candy, they also accepted her. The candy served both a practical and symbolic function for this girl; tossing her a "lifesaver" kept her alive long enough so that she could learn how to swim. Much later she revealed a vow she had made never to attach herself to anyone other than her biological mother. A very supportive adoptive parent was able to locate the biological mother and the girl eventually reconnected with her family. The Lifesavers became a tradition between her and her therapist, a concrete example that a special bond joined them. Seven years later the girl still keeps in touch with her therapist and has a relatively stable personal life.

Enrichment

To counter the children's view that the world is withholding and austere, we want to present a view that relationships between adults and children can be bountiful and gratifying. Food is an obvious first step to changing their world view. By providing treats, sweets, toys, and other pleasures, the clinicians provide enough direct narcissistic gratification for the children to start building positive relationships with the adults. This process draws the children into treatment.

Many people seem uncomfortable with the concept that to recuperate, deprived children benefit from being indulged The typical objections are often put in medical terms— sweets cause hyperactivity, weight gain, tooth decay— but are more likely to be morally based.

The National Academy of Sciences states that a very small group of children are sensitive to food additives produced from coal tar derivatives. Other than this small group, most studies have shown that sweets or other foods do not cause hyperactivity except in special circumstances. On one hand, many of these children are quite small for their age at the start of treatment (psychosocial dwarfism is common), and they do put on weight disproportionately to their growth in height. They do need to be reminded to brush their teeth. On the other hand, with food that pleases them, they are much happier, which facilitates their emotional recovery. Along with their improved mood, the children are less irritable, so they find self-control easier.

Moral objections to gratification usually are based either on a concern that indulgence fosters unrealistic expectations or the fear that these children will never be satisfied. Give them a finger and they will want an arm. We have found neither to be the case. Typically the children focus on oral gratification for the first month or two. Like the infant, with time and continuing gratification the children learn to associate gratification with the gratifier, which is the precursor to human connectedness. Eventually the children come to trust that food will be there regularly. A sense of security that there will be enough for everyone replaces the drive to fill up, and the children become calmer and more able to share.

We have been told anecdotally that after World War II a

group of orphan children rescued from a concentration camp were placed in an American residential treatment center. They stole food nightly. The child care staff began to set out a table full of food every night. After a short time the stealing stopped and the children began to thrive. Later, as the children gained confidence, this ritual was no longer needed.

Although food is basic and usually is the first form of gratification the children will accept, they can be nurtured in many other ways. The clinicians need to find whatever ways the children will like and accept as the place to start. Providing a warm cozy blanket or a stuffed animal, or singing a special song may begin the process. These children value the adult's ability to fix broken toys and repair torn clothing. They appreciate the metaphor that damaged goods can be repaired.

Initially the children will be wary. Life has given them good reason to be. Although physical and emotional hunger will drive the children to accept food or nurturance, fear, mistrust, and guilt will make some children hesitant to accept good things. Some will expect that they will have to repay kind treatment with sexual favors. Others will not want to admit that they want something, and thus risk being hurt. Some will want to avoid vulnerability. If you feed from a hand, you may be less free to bite it in self-defense. Children may test the program's therapeutic attitudes and intentions many times before freely accepting food or caring.

Eventually, maltreated children no longer need the treats, although the adults are well advised to continue providing them until the children themselves say that treats can be stopped. Then the children find themselves looking forward to seeing favorite staff members, and feeling happier and enthusiastic about the day's activities. First, the children learn to turn to people to get physical gratification. Then they learn that people can provide psychological gratification. Much later, when the heart is closer to being healed, pleasure in relationships with human beings becomes a goal in itself.

Their intense and often unspoken sense of alienation, the notion that they are from outer space or less than human, slowly starts to give way to a slightly more positive view. It took months of work for one child to say, "The world sucks, but you're OK– sometimes."

On Being Special and Valued

Children thrive in an environment in which they are to a certain degree pampered and indulged. Even doing this symbolically tells the children, "We think you are special." Many programs that deal with deprived children would say that they work sensitively to heal their clients' wounds. Unfortunately, we have found that many programs approach the children with the attitude, "Life is unfair; you need to shape up and accept it." Although everyone must eventually accept what is unfair in life, forcing these children, who have been through the most terrible experiences, to accept this perspective early in their treatment is, in reality, to refuse to come to grips with their rage and pain. If the children acquiesce, they may learn to suppress their anger to avoid retribution. But the rage remains inside, often just below the surface.

An alternative is to accept that the children have valid, understandable reasons for feeling as they do, and to take the clinical stance that says, "I understand that life has been very unfair to you. To the extent that I am able to, I will make restitution." Naturally, many therapists resist the notion that taking even indirect responsibility for acts of adults who have treated the children so poorly can be therapeutic. They feel it will provoke the children to lash out against the treatment team. That has not been our experience. The key point is that when the children first enter the treatment program, they are unable to differentiate between adult figures. In the children's mind, all adults are in cahoots against them; all treat children badly. Although the compensation the clinicians provide is at best symbolic, and in reality quite limited compared to what these children have been through, it presents the children with a more positive view of human relationships. The children can then begin to consider making the psychological adjustments that would permit them to move beyond their previous trauma. Indeed, the children's ability to distinguish adults who hurt from those who help marks a major step in the therapeutic process.

An 11-year-old boy recounted how his older stepbrother had forcibly sodomized him while the 11-year-old was visiting his mother. At first his mother had refused to believe him. After the stepbrother admitted to the act, the mother blamed the 11-year-old for what had happened. After all, he had been the one to visit.

As the boy described the events, the clinician realized that his mother's reaction had been even more traumatic than the rape itself. The boy's pain and sense of outrage moved the therapist, who explained that he could not undo the injury. But he could apologize for the terrible treatment the boy had received. As symbolic compensation, he gave the boy, "on behalf of the adults of the world," a small toy the boy had wanted. The boy never referred to the sodomization directly again, but made frequent reference to "the stuff we talked about in your office," and how good he felt about the talk. He saw the therapist as an ally, and never held him responsible for the violation.

When compensation can be linked to the abuser, the experience can be even more therapeutic. A teenage girl, who had made several suicide attempts, refused to talk to her father at all. Finally she told him how his psychological intimidation and cruel punishments had terrified her. Realizing that his daughter's criticism was accurate, the father accepted responsibility, explained that he had a terrible childhood, and really knew little about how to be a good father. With the therapist's encouragement, he said that he wished he could provide "compensation for her injury." The girl was asked to list the wrongs and define what she felt was fair compensation. After much thought, she said that compensation was not necessary. She just wanted her father not to do such things in the future. Although much work remained to be done; that meeting represented a positive step in their relationship and in the girl's progress.

Stability in Human Relationships and Program

These children's personal relationships have been so chaotic that they need stable human relationships to recover. Day-to-day experiences with the same persons help these children organize their chaotic feelings into a more stable internal state. As much as possible, the same people should deal with them every day. Through living together and solving mundane issues, the children and caregivers come to know each other and to recognize the subtle but important ways each reacts— the particular ways each conveys moods, shows joy and distress, thinks. Being treated as individuals with unique responses helps the children structure their personalities and begins to undercut their conviction that they are throwaways. No matter how consistent program policy is, it is the personal element that makes the difference. Having to deal with multiple caregivers is somewhat akin to having a babysitter or substitute teacher— adequate supervision may be provided, the tasks may be accomplished, but the personal connection is tentative. This tentativeness is antithetical to the treatment goal because it does not provide an emotionally secure base and reduce the children's anxiety.

As the children start to attach to adults, the program must take care to respect this process. Developing relationships takes time, and is not linear with these children. A child may speak openly and intimately with a staff figure one day, and then precipitate a crisis the next, perhaps in response to the anxiety that closeness and trust brought. Therapists and caretakers may be uncomfortable both with the long-term responsibility that goes with this process and with the anger and frustration that comes from a child who had seemed to be building a relationship and then blew up. The adults must take extra care to follow through on commitments so as to preserve the fragile trust a child is developing. This may involve hunting for a toy or record the child considers special, or making extra efforts to respond to a unique need.

A boy asked for Dastardly Mash ice cream, but the adult could only find butter pecan at the store, so she bought that. When the boy continued to be antagonistic to her, she felt betrayed and hurt that the boy should fail to appreciate her efforts to nurture him. Later she reviewed the situation with colleagues and realized that she had responded only to the boy's need for ice cream, but had disregarded his trusting her with a specific request. In this way he was not so different from anyone else. Who wants butter pecan when you love Dastardly Mash? But this boy was particularly sensitive to the slight implied when his request was treated as generic. When the adult got him Dastardly Mash, the situation and their relationship improved somewhat.

Similarly, clinicians must make sure that they keep appointments promptly, for these children find waiting for key figures unbearable. If a clinician is late for an appointment, the child may feel intensely that "I can't count on y ou." It creates more stress and internal tension than these children can bear. Not infrequently it leads to explosive outbursts. One teenager explained the situation explicitly: "Don't you realize how important you are to me? You're the only thing between me and death. When you're late I get frightened that you're dead or don't want to see me. I can't stand it!"

Dependency and Separation

Some people find these children's intense dependency unbearable. In our opinion, that may be one reason why some people in child welfare and mental health argue that in our world of limited resources, deprived and maltreated children cannot be helped to develop stable relationships. They may point out that in their experience, children who develop a meaningful relationship have a hard time leaving a program after the children and adults get attached to each other. This approach is similar to arguing that we should not feed babies if they are hungry because they will only grow larger and keep demanding more food.

A better solution would be to pay more attention to separations, using the feelings that short absences and later termination arouse as a crucial part of the learning process that treatment is. These children may understand that in everyday life, brief separations are unavoidable, but they still are extremely vulnerable and experience great anxiety and distress during these periods. Therefore, to the extent possible, the adults must protect the children from the overwhelming anxiety and subsequent behavioral problems that can come with even relatively short separations. Sometimes an act as simple as explaining and reviewing the upcoming schedules of child care workers' can help reassure children about when key adults will return.

The behavior of many children deteriorated while their therapists were away on vacation. Therefore the program director developed a policy in which children whose therapists were away were given extra treats and attention after the therapist departed. The children were told in this way that the program was acknowledging their distress, and demonstrating its desire to be nice to them when they felt abandoned. This approach helped the children span the vacation period with less regression in their behavior. That made them easier for the adults to live with, emphasized the program's belief that human relationships were important, and encouraged the children to stick with their relationships even if it caused them intermittent pain.

Clinicians are wise to provide concrete ways that help the children bind their anxiety and contain their inner tension when separation is necessary. Many of these children do not have any faith or expectation that figures will reappear once they leave; important people in their lives have abandoned them forever. As a partial remedy, the children might be allowed to hold some personal object that belongs to the adult as a talisman that reassures them that the lost person will return. Many clinicians know that getting mail is an exciting and rare event for any child so they send the children letters or postcards while they are away. These postcards are cherished partly because they provide concrete reassurance that the children are not being completely abandoned, rejected or forgotten, and also because they say that the children are important enough that the adult would take the time to think of the child when away. Photographs of favorite adults can also reassure children during separations.

An intensely depressed teenage girl became suicidal when her therapist was unavailable on weekends. She believed that the therapist had left her for good and would not reappear on Monday. After some time, she described how her mother would disappear from their home erratically in response to her father's violent outbursts. The girl would wake up some mornings and find her mother gone. She had no idea where the mother was, nor could she predict when or whether her mother would return. Once the adults understood the girl's dilemma, they worked with the child on a special weekend plan that provided additional support during the vulnerable period.

Since many children secretly fear when they are being discharged that it is because the program has found them to be unworthy and wants to get rid of them, the adults must make an extra effort to reassure them. At shorter-term diagnostic centers or hospital units, where the goal may be to diagnose, initiate treatment, and prepare children for longer-term treatment, children handle the transition better if they feel that the adults are sincerely looking out for their interests and have made good plans for them. Preplacement visits that provide opportunities to meet and talk with key adults and children in the new foster home or residential placement help make the transition less stressful.

Concrete objects can become magical in that they help to provide security during the move. Like the two-year old's security blanket, these objects symbolize adult caring and constancy amidst change. Special "Goodbye Books," individually designed and assembled for each child and containing pictures, memorabilia, and written notes from friends the child has made, can be helpful. As a transition, the child can be given a bag filled with special small toys, treats, and activities to open only after coming to the new setting.

In these transitions the clinicians can also take concrete steps to make the system work better for the child. Since formal clinical summaries rarely have information that the child care staff is most interested in, child care workers in the two programs will benefit from speaking directly to each other. To help the child feel welcomed and more at home, the child care staff in the old program can give specific instructions to the new workers about the child's favorite interests, eating and bedtime needs, idiosyncratic ways of coping with anxiety, and the like. To ease the transition, key figures may visit the child after the move, both to let the child know they care and to discuss the child's needs and situation with workers in the new program.

A teenage girl on an evaluation unit was extremely apprehensive about an upcoming transfer to a longer-term program in another community. Staff members who had worked in similar programs told her what these programs were like, what rules and daily schedules she could expect, and what advantages her new, less restrictive living situation would provide. On the day before her discharge, the adults organized a party. Several other children decorated the room and baked brownies. Key staff people and community friends attended. In what amounted to a graduation ceremony, they exchanged special goodbye gifts with her. Later the girl said that the party was the first time she had said goodbye to people who she felt were not trying to get rid of her. Feeling good about her departure facilitated her entry into the new program.

Children in relatively stable, well-organized homes use routines to help them feel secure. When they are anxious, they can retreat to favorite toys kept in special places; when the time comes for bed, a defined ritual helps in the transition. With time, this predictability is internalized and becomes an important element in modulating anxiety. Even small changes in routine, particularly if they are unannounced, may distress children, because the changes emphasize how small, vulnerable, and helpless a child is.

External order is necessary for children to develop internal order. A therapeutic milieu aims to achieve the same end that routines and predictability do for children raised in competent homes. The child who has lived in a chaotic environment has not had the opportunity to develop these internal mechanisms. Therefore, the program aims to provide external order so the children begin to develop internal means to soothe distress and to stimulate the ability to defer action, so they will be able to think before acting. These aims make a stable, understanding, and understandable program crucial. Much progress that children make in institutional treatment does not result from brilliant therapy, but rather from the simple fact that the children's day is structured intelligently

For years, a father brutalized his wife and 13-year-old daughter. Finally the wife killed him; the daughter witnessed the death. During multiple placements the girl developed serious behavioral problems until she was finally placed in an inpatient psychiatric unit. She did relatively well until the program director initiated a change without adequately preparing the staff members or the children. The girl threw a temper tantrum, and announced that she was" fed up with changes." She then described in vivid detail the seven different places she had lived in during the three months following her father's murder, and how angry she was about so many changes in her life. The director accepted responsibility, apologized to both the child care staff and the children for his error, and canceled the change. This calmed her and the child care staff members, who had been faced with the unpleasant task of forcing the children to accept an undesired change in routine. The program director established a special work group consisting of child care workers and children, explained the administrative need, and allowed the group to examine several possible program changes and think about how they might affect the group. The group came up with a plan that was understood, accepted, and carried out successfully.

In contrast, children typically respond extremely well to sudden changes forced by emergency. For example, when a child needs urgent medical care, the other children usually remain on their best behavior throughout the emergency, even though fewer adults may be around to supervise them. When the other children see how the adults drop everything to respond to a child in desperate need, they are reassured that if they should have a similar emergency need, the staff would respond to it immediately with the same care and concern. This builds a sense of security.

Contact with Parents

In recent years child welfare advocates have been increasingly concerned about children getting lost in the social welfare system and remaining in foster care indefinitely. These concerns have refocused the goals of treatment to returning children to their families. Clinicians have recognized that keeping the family involved in treatment helps obtain and maintain their cooperation. It also helps provide information about the family's current status, and prepares the family for the time the children will be leaving group care.

It may remedy situations that caused the child's disturbance. Some families have the desire and ability to participate in treatment. Family therapy or various forms of conjoint parent-training programs have been found to be useful in helping families to cope more constructively and have helped free many children from a scapegoat role.

Although returning children home is a worthy goal in many cases, it is unrealistic and destructive in others. Parents of seriously mistreated children are often rejecting, unpredictable, and immature, if not overtly dangerous to their children. Without the clinician moderating and stabilizing the family meetings, the parent-child relationship often careens wildly out of control. To allow a child to return home to such a situations would be irresponsible and could undermine gains made in years of residential treatment. Family therapy is not a panacea with this population. There are hazards and limitations in its use.[2] Even those parents who are willing to maintain contact may be hard to engage constructively in the treatment process because they have deep-seated difficulties dealing with authority figures.

Few parents are grateful that the state has declared them unfit and removed their children. The children are bounced about on a sea of conflicting loyalties and confused feelings. Parental ambivalence toward the treatment process, perhaps coupled with personal disorganization, poverty, and/or drug or alcohol use, may make it hard for parents to keep appointments. When parents fail to appear for scheduled meetings, children sink into great anxiety about their safety or are plunged into great anger and subsequent guilt over what they experience as a rejection. To protect the children and the program from the overwhelming anxiety and subsequent behavioral problems that may come if the parents are late for a visit, clinicians may find it safest to tell children that parents are scheduled to visit sometime later in the day rather than telling them when the actual appointment is.

Parents may lie to clinicians or children; they may overtly

or covertly oppose the goals of treatment and thus undermine the process. Parents may encourage the child to settle peer problems through violence at the same time the program is trying to promote verbal approaches. They may pressure children not to testify in court or not to reveal information about family secrets, in order to protect other family members or hide illicit activity from the law. They may show their children an unstable pattern, enticing them at one moment and rejecting them the next, depending on their momentary emotional state, blood alcohol level, or current life situation. Children find this erratic pattern confusing and infuriating.

Commonly these children are dragged into marital conflicts or postdivorce battles. Often, parents, because they feel guilty, make unrealistic or overly optimistic promises to the child, or make excessive demands of the treatment program. They may visit children while drunk or under the influence of drugs, which embarrasses the children.

Many parents, however, are seriously committed to their children. Despite severe problems these parents show great concern for their children's welfare, and may be very grateful for the opportunities treatment provides their children. As one parent put it, "I don't know how to be a good parent—I never had one. Teach me, I want to learn. I don't want my child to go through what I went through."

Given this wide range of parental attitudes and capabilities, what should a treatment program do about interactions between parents and children? That depends on the specific parents and the treatment goals. If the immediate clinical task is to stabilize the child in his or her current living situation, and the clinicians judge that parental contact will seriously interfere with that task, the need to limit that contact is obvious. In some situations, contact between a parent and a child is clearly dangerous because it can provoke extreme anxiety or anger, potentially compromising the child's or parent's tenuous self-control over assaultive, suicidal, or homicidal behavior.

A mother phoned her suicidal 13-year-old daughter. During the conversation, she asked her daughter to leave the program to join her in jumping off the Golden Gate Bridge. She tried to persuade the daughter to keep the request secret, but the daughter told the child care staff, who rapidly alerted the child's therapist. The therapist contacted the mother immediately and was able to persuade her to accept psychiatric hospitalization voluntarily.

Cautious contact with parents is useful for diagnostic purposes and for long-term planning. Often, placement aims to assess parents' and children's capacity to successfully get along and ultimately to live together. In some situations, the parent may become an active ally in the treatment process, supporting and participating in the children's care. In these cases, extended contact allows the parent to monitor the child's progress and may help the parent learn more about good parenting. It also may help allay parental fears that the child might again be maltreated.

Children with no parents or surrogates present an even more difficult clinical problem. Since these children are so extraordinarily alone, they often are depressed and bitter. To protect themselves from the terrible abandonment they have suffered, they often deny that they need human relationships. To work with them, the therapist has to be far more active, giving more as a real person to make up for the deficit and to entice them into a therapeutic relationship.

An adopted teenage girl with a long history of a hostile-dependent relationship pattern was rejected again. Her adoptive parents successfully petitioned the court to set aside the adoption, arguing that their daughter was already mentally ill when she was adopted at five. Subsequently the girl was depressed for a long time. She ultimately went to live in a long-term group home, but kept in active contact with her therapist by letter. She explained that having someone she could tell about her progress helped her feel better.

The Construction of Positive Identifications

Not surprisingly, some of these children feel both intense anger and deep longing. After all, their parents, toward whom they have a natural, biological attachment, are the people who have mistreated them. But their anger is so intense, and the fear that they will lose control and strike out is so strong, that adults are frightened. For example, for years a stepfather beat his stepson and forced him to watch the stepfather sexually abuse the boy's sister. When the boy was asked what he would want to say to the mistreating stepparent, he responded, "I'm going to kill you." A sensitive clinician would not be surprised that this rage would influence and shape this boy's dealings with other adult authority figures, such as teachers and probation officers. But this boy was physically large and potentially explosive, so the adults were concerned about their own and other children's safety. As a means of strengthening his controls and dealing with the anxiety he produced in the adults, it was tempting to threaten to transfer the boy to a juvenile detention center if he hit anyone. The boy protested against the threat, saying that he had done nothing untoward. Such threats only made him more anxious because they resembled the threats his father had made. Some intervention was needed to break the mutual distrust. The boy, child care staff, and therapist met together and developed a plan. All agreed that if either adult or child was feeling anxious about a loss of control, this would be identified quickly and immediate steps would be taken to defuse the situation. A series of measures that the boy could use to help strengthen his controls were identified and agreed upon. The child care staff was alert to the need to approach the boy without intimidating him. They suggested that when he felt stressed he either talk it over with some staff member or if he was unable to do this, that he withdraw to his room and rest on his bed. The boy was also allowed to use tranquilizers to calm himself if necessary when his tension became too great. The plan was periodically reassessed and revisions were made as his situation changed. This arrangement enabled the boy to finish initial treatment successfully and to go to live in a group home, where he received continued treatment and did well.

Another boy, described as explosive and paranoid, had been through similar experiences. He said, "All an adult has to do is sound like my father, or raise his forehead like my father used to, and I get so angry I want to kill him."

But this anger is not isolated or independent from the children's intense longing. Just beneath these children's anger lies a sense of bitterness and deprivation that is stimulated and intensified every time they are reminded that they do not have what other children do. Watching a TV program that shows a father and son having a good time, or hearing other children talk about positive experiences with their parents, stimulates the feelings of loss, jealousy, and anger. Coupled with this is self-hatred. This hatred is the child's internalization of attitudes the mistreating parents held and often communicated directly to the child. After all, these children are no-good scum, worthless bastards who belong in hell.[3]

When one therapist actually started crying and telling an abandoned eight-year-old girl she would miss her, the girl kept insisting that the therapist was trying to deceive her. But she quickly and proudly told other people, who she had thought would be glad to be rid of her, "Do you know what my therapist did? She cried because I was leaving."

Since these children suffer from fundamentally and profoundly distorted relationships with adults, treatment must involve creating relationships in which adult authority figures are constructive. Rather than being sadistic, rejecting, and self-centered, the new authority figures accept, nurture, and protect the children both physically and psychologically; are sympathetic towards the children's legitimate needs as the children define them; and must be powerful enough to convey strength and to command respect. Ultimately the power comes from superior reason rather than physical ability, for the clinicians show the children that they can apply this reasoning to solve problems that stymie the children and to control anxieties that cripple them.

A father had severely mistreated his nine-year-old son from the time the boy was two until he divorced when his son was five. The boy apparently did well until age eight, when his grandparent, a positive, protecting figure to the boy, died. As the boy grew more anxious and depressed, he had intrusive thoughts that his sadistic father was returning to beat or kill him. He became more irritable and frightened, started carrying a weapon, and began getting into serious fights at school. His fears reached delusional proportions. In treatment, the therapist, in addition to using medication, wisely focused on constructing a strong positive male relationship, stressing that a good father would want to help the boy build models, protect him from danger, and support his interest in rock music. The boy, who was bright, said that when he started to feel frightened, he would think about the good times he was having with the therapist and make plans for the next day. Over time, the boy recovered.

Setting Limits

Since encouraging a more comfortable life together and avoiding unnecessary frustrations are paramount, setting limits becomes a difficult problem. With careful thought and additional effort, many confrontations can be avoided, as illustrated in the following considerations.

As much as possible the rules ought to come from a mutual effort that the staff and peer group engage in together, rather than being imposed arbitrarily from above. Discussing what rules make communal life more comfortable with the entire group facilitates this process.

When staff members have to turn down some request, they ought to show the children as much respect as possible in the process of saying no, because every rejection is a slight. The focus should always be on the adults' wanting to respond to the children's desires; the external reasons that prevent the adults from responding should be explained. Whenever possible, the adult should propose an alternative that might be almost as useful to the child. An independent child's request for assistance is a major step forward and should be treated with care. This style emphasizes our desire to preserve the positive relationship we are trying to build.

Adults slip easily from the respectful tone we might use with a spouse, fellow worker, or superior into a command style that emphasizes, "I am the boss!" or "Do it because I say so!" Such a tone runs the risk of arousing old feelings about authority figures. Some rules obviously are essential for safety and cannot be compromised; usually the group understands this. Indeed, the group may be reassured that the adults are caring and sensible enough to assure the children's safety, and will not be bullied into compromising on these issues.

Many assumptions adults make to justify their rules are unknown to children; occasionally they are also unknown to the adults. Staff members should frequently take time out from busy schedules to stop the action, and, in terms the children can understand, discuss why they think certain issues are important. If their logic is flawed and the child persuades them that he or she has a better way to deal with the issue than the means the adults have suggested, why not accept the child's suggestion? What could more persuasively bolster the child's self-esteem?

The adults must be in control of themselves. They have to be firm without using threats or increasing passions that escalate the level of conflict. To paraphrase Freud, "The voice of reason is soft, but insistent." Living by reason keeps the anxiety level down and models a process we want the children to experience and internalize.

The adults should try to avoid coercion. It rapidly uses up the good will they have worked so hard to create.

Most adults would think these children would accept this relationship warmly. Actually the children may find it quite confusing because a constructive relationship is so contrary to their expectations. Initially they may see the adults as wimpy or weak for refusing to fight. In response to this internal confusion they may retreat from the process or consciously test the adults to see how they handle certain thorny situations.

After several years of frequent coercive molestation, a teenage girl attempted suicide. As soon as she met with her therapist, she bragged about her ability to please men and demanded that he engage in oral sex with her. When he declined, she threatened to leave the session, saying that if he did not accept her in that way, she had no worth and was better off dead. The therapist explained that he was concerned about her but did not believe that another sexual relationship would help her. Rather, he wanted to have a relationship where she was valued as a human being, rather than because she was able to please him sexually. Although she was furious that he had refused her offer, she reluctantly admitted that she found it hard to believe that people could have nonsexual relationships. Weeks later she confessed that she had hoped that the therapist would say no, but had to make sure.

A ten-year-old-boy whose stepfather had abused him subsequently sodomized his half-sister. He entered treatment when he became suicidal. Soon after entering a residential treatment setting, he flew into a rage and tore a giant stuffed animal while cursing a child care worker. For 30 minutes he sat about ten feet from the worker while she sewed up the animal. During this time the child continuously cursed the worker, using every foul term he knew. He then said he felt much better and wanted to go back to class. Many weeks later he explained that the foul terms he had used were expressions his stepfather had used when hitting him. He asked why the animal was being repaired, saying that he would only wind up tearing it again the next time he was angry. The child care worker told him that she was glad that he hurt a stuffed animal and not himself. Since fixing the animal had helped the boy feel better she didn't mind sewing it. In the next ten weeks, the boy damaged the animal about 15 times, with gradually decreasing frequency.

The same boy had repetitive nightmares that he attributed to episodes in which his stepfather, while drunk, had come into his room at night and had choked him. The boy believed that only his mother's intervention had prevented him from being killed. After he left the home, he would go though a ritual before going to bed. The only thing he would accept from adults was stuffed animals. Ultimately he acquired over 500. Every night, for protection, he circled his bed with his army of stuffed animals. Over time, his nightmares decreased and he no longer wanted to kill himself. He became less aggressive, but retained a cold, detached, and somewhat sadistic style of dealing with the world.

Maltreated children's confusion and distancing from adults gradually give way to a demanding expectation that important adults be there all the time. The relationship with the adults has become truly important to the children. Their brave independence has given way. Now they acknowledge that they need and want human contact. In an attempt to respond to years of unmet need, a child may become clinging and possessive in the relationship. This elicits a commitment that sometimes worries adults. The relationship and commitment need to be kept for the child to get better. But the adult will be internalized, outgrown, and let go of eventually.

One child wanted to buy something in a store, and when the clinician accompanied her, the child could not decide what exactly she wanted. She changed her mind several times and went back and forth among the displays. Eventually she grew angry at herself because she was indecisive. The adult followed patiently, making occasional supportive comments, and eventually paying for the item the child chose. Once outside, the child asked, "Why are you so nice to me? I mean, why do you put up with me? " Then, answering her own question, she said, "You must really like me. I don't think I like myself as much as you like me."

The same child asked the clinician to help her buy medicine for her pet. When the adult agreed, the child exclaimed, "I knew you would help! When something is really important to me, you find some way to help. You're the only person that's ever treated me that way, and that's why you're the only person I like. I like my pet a lot more than I like people."

Over time, the positive figures, the positive experiences, and the adults' positive regard for and empathy with the children begin to be incorporated into each child's world. The good present experiences allow them to acquire some psychological distance from the damage previous mistreatment has created. Experience, identification, and incorporation take time and cannot be forced or speeded beyond the pace the children can tolerate, which is why therapeutic placement may require many years to restore a child to health.

As the children feel more secure, their previous experiences are no longer so overwhelmingly disturbing. The good has tempered what the bad has done. When the present is so much better, it is harder to be enraged full-time about the past. Voluntarily, the children start to talk more about their past maltreatment, often comparing the past with the present. Although at this time, discussing previous events is useful to the children and may help them develop a better understanding and perspective about the bad times, discussing the past usually occurs late in the treatment. However, as the children begin to tell in stark detail what they have actually experienced, the clinicians may find it painful to hear what a child they like has suffered through.[4]

The mental image of the positive figures, the memory of the experiences with benevolent authority, can be an extraordinarily powerful sustaining experience. It can serve as an antidote to trauma and mistreatment. Throughout their lives, people return to such experiences and memories to restore their sense of meaning and value in life in the face of adversity.

Developing Nonviolent Behavior

For these children, the process of developing internal controls is slow and gradual. It is connected as much to the improvement in their mood as it is related to learning and wanting to use ways other than violence to solve problems.

During a violent episode, the adults' alternatives are quite limited. If children are injuring someone else or themselves, the adults must control the situation, even if this entails being coercive— pulling the children apart if they are fighting, holding a child if he or she is punching someone, and so forth. If a child is being destructive to property, the adults have a little more flexibility, depending on what exact damage is being inflicted. In such situations, the child most likely is frustrated because he or she sees no way to get needs met; the child feels hurt and thus angry, or feels threatened and is acting aggressively for self-protection.

Often the children's reluctance or inability to communicate needs causes the frustration that leads to a violent outburst. The reluctance stems from the belief that adults will neither listen nor be helpful, a lesson they learned at home. The children's inability may develop because they lack an emotional vocabulary, a deficit resulting from an upbringing where children's feelings were neither defined nor demarcated. Because they do not trust adults, they try to solve problems on their own, but often they lack the skill and ability to do so. Such children, given some hard math problems to do, will not say to their teacher, "This is too hard. I need some help." Rather, they will think, "I can't do these problems. I'm dumb. I hate myself and I hate them for making me feel this way." Then the child crumples the paper and throws it across the room. Adults who see only the paper being thrown might conclude that these children are simply challenging authority, rather than making a statement about themselves, their frustration, and their pessimism. The children believe that no solution exists for their seemingly hopeless predicament.

The second reason for the violent behavior is that the children feel hurt and angry and want revenge. Some adults assume that these children become angry for no reason, which eliminates the need to examine what is happening in the immediate life situation that irritates them. Irritability often goes hand in hand with depression and being overwhelmed. All of us are familiar with times we have had to deal with too much, with trying to function when we are too stressed. When we are in such a tense frame of mind, even small frustrations, which normally would not bother us, can lead to blow-ups. In some circumstances it takes only one additional straw to break the camel's back; with thought, the adults learn to recognize when the camel is fully loaded and add no more straw.

A seven-year-old boy with a history of fire-setting had been doing relatively well. With no notice, he began destroying his room and screaming at the child care workers. Finally he had to be restrained. His therapist could not figure out why this had happened. At an interdisciplinary staffing, the child care workers pointed out that this boy's friend was about to leave and that the boy did not have a good relationship with any other children in the group, who were all older. The workers suggested a plan whereby the boy received additional individual attention at times during the day to help him deal with his loneliness and anxiety. This plan worked well. In reviewing the episode, the boy commented, "Well, at least I didn't set fire to anything."

Still another reason for attacking is to defend oneself against attack. At times children are scared—perhaps panicky would be a better term—and they attack first. Since the treating adults consider themselves well intentioned, they may find it had to believe that children can be scared of them and see them as malevolent. But adults are far larger than most of these children and can do many unpleasant things. Further, the children are well aware that compared to adults they are relatively powerless. The many times they have been hit in the past have demonstrated this fact.

When stressed with a situation close to an old trauma, some children may start to relive the traumatic episode and completely lose contact with the current situation. A 14-year-old girl was angry about a disagreement with her therapist and started pounding on the window of her room. When a large staff member came into the room and started to restrain her, she became panicky and terrified and ultimately required medication. In reviewing the episode with her therapist she said, "You don't understand. It wasn't "like my father was holding me down." It *was* my father holding me down."

The best, but difficult, therapeutic strategy in such situations is to do the minimum necessary to protect life and limb, and to assume that some therapeutic error or slight provoked the child to anger. If the clinician asks, "What are we doing wrong to make you so angry?" many times the child will give an answer that helps the adult to better understand the situation. With this information the adult can help the child to develop a more adaptive response and find a more fruitful way to get what he or she needs.

In more peaceful moments, the adults can look at their overall relationship with such a child and ask, "Can I do anything to make the child happier? Does the child have some need that we are failing to hear? Are we, in some way that we don't fully understand, frightening the child and provoking an attack in response?" Just asking these questions can point towards therapeutic responses that reduce future violence. Paying close attention to the child's behavior and to our own attitudes, and using our insight to help the child achieve his or her ends are the best deterrents to violence and other forms of acting out. Simultaneously, the child is learning to see adults as helpful individuals who are understanding and occasionally can be trusted, thus increasing his or her range of prosocial, nonviolent responses to frustration.

DEVELOPING AN IDENTITY

Ordinarily, as part of normal child-rearing, parents observe and acknowledge children's feelings and views about day-to-day living. From infancy, parents sense who their child is as an individual and develop mutual interactions based on this conception. Thus a mother, when feeding an infant, will remark about the child's preferences and propensities— "She likes to be held this way" or "He likes spaghetti but hates soft-boiled eggs." This sensitivity allows the child to develop as a psychological entity distinct from the parents—the child is allowed to develop a sense that he or she is an individual.

Much has been written about separation-individuation as it normally occurs, and how this process stimulates and allows normal personality development. We wish to reiterate only that individuation is not limited to a particular phase of childhood but rather occurs throughout maturation. Consider first the process of a parent feeding a one-year-old. A good-enough parent is capable of saying, "I like carrots but my child likes peas. I will feed my child peas and she will be happy." In contrast, consider the extreme situation in which the parent says, "I like carrots. Carrots are what children must like. My child will eat carrots even if it means I have to force them into her mouth and hold it shut to make her swallow."

A child raised in the latter situation fails to develop a clear sense of connection between the biological/neurological pleasure centers and eating, because eating is no longer pleasurable. If, as Freud said, "The first ego is a body ego," it is no surprise that such a child has ego deficits.

Consider also the experience of an eight-year-old youngster who comes home from school. Normal parents usually ask the children about their day, what they enjoyed, what was interesting, and the like. The process encourages children to define their feelings, to delineate needs, and to refine perspectives about their life experience.

However, if parents continually voice suicidal ideation, for example, the children are forced to focus on the parents' psychological needs and to be anxious about the parents' well-being. The children neither go through the process of developing personal definition, nor do they develop the view that their personal views have value. The damage to the children's personality is subtle but real; it becomes profound when the pattern is repeated daily over time. In comparison to normal children, these children are often unable to let another know who they are, since they are so uncertain themselves. This deficit makes it much harder to understand them. If the adults pay careful attention to the children's preferences and feelings, respecting them as important, and offering them the opportunity for choices within the range of their capabilities, the children's identity development will be stimulated. The clinician must be alert not to confuse adults' feelings and needs with the children's feelings and needs, particularly with compliant children who may have mastered the art of making others comfortable as a way to survive.

Summary

The therapeutic challenge the initial treatment period presents is to make enough human contact and connection with these children so that they will be able to survive and benefit from further treatment that addresses their aberrant personality patterns. In our experience, an approach that acknowledges the extraordinary trauma these children have endured is the best way to establish this initial connection with them. This understanding enables the clinicians, both child care workers and therapists, to develop a prescriptive approach that stimulates them to build human relationships. For these children, the good-enough experience and positive relationships counteract the trauma and form a base for continued exploration and growth.

If we are to live in a more humane, safe society we must understand these children better. The wounds they have suffered as children return to haunt all of us if they become violent or antisocial adults. If our society would expend more money on healing these wounds, each of us might be able to walk the streets more safely and to sleep better at night. The ultimate selfish act would be for all of us to recognize that healing disturbed and disturbing children's hearts would help each of us heal many fears and anxieties. For these children are not another species. There but for the grace of God go you and I.

Notes

1 Again, see Lenore Terr's work.

2 Weitzman, Jack, "Engaging the Severely Dysfunctional Family in Treatment: Basic Considerations," *Family Process* 24 (1985): 473–485.

3 See Garabino, J.; Guttman, E.; and Seeley, J.W., *The Psychologically Battered Child* (San Francisco, CA: Jossey-Bass, 1987), for an excellent discussion of the issues relating to emotional abuse.

4 Kessler and Rosenfeld (1989) are exploring the issue of these resistances.

V

About the Authors

Alvin Rosenfeld, M.D., is Director of Psychiatric Services, Jewish Child Care Association, and Senior Research Scholar, Columbia University's Elbenwood Center for the Study of Family as Educator. He was educated at Cornell University and at Harvard Medical School, where he also trained in psychiatry and child psychiatry. Prior to moving to New York City, he was on the faculty at Harvard Medical School, then served as director of child psychiatry training at Stanford University Medical School. Dr. Rosenfeld is one of the six academic advisors on the Children's Advertising Review Unit of the Better Business Bureau. He is the author of over sixty professional publications, dealing primarily with child abuse and neglect, and child rearing in "typical" families, and with his wife, Dr. Dorothy Levine, writes a regular column on child rearing for *American Baby* Magazine.

Saul Wasserman, M.D., is Medical Director, Pacific Center for Child and Adolescent Behavioral Medicine, San Jose Medical Center, and Clinical Associate Professor of Child Psychiatry, Stanford University. A native of New York, he attended Cornell University, graduating with a degree in Engineering Physics. His medical training was at the University of Chicago School of Medicine and his training in psychiatry at Stanford University. He has served as a consultant to many governmental agencies in the fields of child abuse and child mental health. In addition to his interest in treatment, Dr. Wasserman is also involved in projects dealing with homeless teenagers, child abuse death review and children's reactions to natural disasters.